Vizsla Dogs

Vizsla Dog Complete Pet Owner's Manual

Vizsla Dog Basics, Choosing and Owning, Breeding, Care, Feeding, Grooming, Showing and Training All Included!

By: Lolly Brown

Copyrights and Trademarks

All rights reserved. No part of this book may be reproduced or transformed in any form or by any means, graphic, electronic, or mechanical, including photocopying, recording, taping, or by any information storage retrieval system, without the written permission of the author.

This publication is Copyright ©2022 NRB Publishing, an imprint of Pack & Post Plus, LLC. Nevada. All products, graphics, publications, software and services mentioned and recommended in this publication are protected by trademarks. In such instance, all trademarks & copyright belong to the respective owners. For information consult www.NRBpublishing.com

Disclaimer and Legal Notice

This product is not legal, medical, or accounting advice and should not be interpreted in that manner. You need to do your own due-diligence to determine if the content of this product is right for you. While every attempt has been made to verify the information shared in this publication, neither the author, neither publisher, nor the affiliates assume any responsibility for errors, omissions or contrary interpretation of the subject matter herein. Any perceived slights to any specific person(s) or organization(s) are purely unintentional.

We have no control over the nature, content and availability of the web sites listed in this book. The inclusion of any web site links does not necessarily imply a recommendation or endorse the views expressed within them. We take no responsibility for, and will not be liable for, the websites being temporarily unavailable or being removed from the internet.

The accuracy and completeness of information provided herein and opinions stated herein are not guaranteed or warranted to produce any particular results, and the advice and strategies, contained herein may not be suitable for every individual. Neither the author nor the publisher shall be liable for any loss incurred as a consequence of the use and application, directly or indirectly, of any information presented in this work. This publication is designed to provide information in regard to the subject matter covered.

Neither the author nor the publisher assume any responsibility for any errors or omissions, nor do they represent or warrant that the ideas, information, actions, plans, suggestions contained in this book is in all cases accurate. It is the reader's responsibility to find advice before putting anything written in this book into practice. The information in this book is not intended to serve as legal, medical, or accounting advice.

Foreword

Welcome! You're about to make a truly wonderful a life-changing journey if you decide to get yourself a Vizsla dog!

If you're considering getting a Vizsla dog to be a part of your family, loving him and then receiving unconditional love in return, you are making a momentous decision.

What's inside this book?

Included inside this book's first section is about the origin and bio of a Vizsla dog. It contains the general information and the characteristics of this specific dog breed.

The Second section is about choosing a Vizsla dog. It tackles about where and how to acquire a Vizsla dog and how to select a healthy Vizsla dog puppy.

The next section will talk about the things that you need and have to do as a Vizsla dog owner.

The fourth section focuses on how you can cater your Vizsla dog's nutritional needs.

The next section delves into basic care and regular grooming needs for your Vizsla dog.

The sixth section is about raising and training your Vizsla dog. It educates dog owners about the importance of training and activities for your dog. It additionally contains a puppy's training outline and guidance in shaping behaviors, training, and problem solving.

Th seventh section focuses on the common health issues of and how to deal with them and respond into emergencies.

Chapter eight is about preparing your Vizsla dog for a dog show.

For the last section, it will talk about the breeding process for your Vizsla dog.

By obtaining this training guide, you will be on your way to securing the necessary tools and knowledge to assure your success as a Vizsla dog owner and trainer.

Table of Contents

Introduction 1

Chapter One: Vizsla Dog Facts and Descriptions 3

    Facts About Vizsla Dogs 3

    Summary of Vizsla Facts 6

    Vizsla Breed History 8

Chapter Two: Choosing and Acquiring a Vizsla Dog 11

    Where to Look For Vizsla Dogs? 11

        Breeders 11

        Rescues 13

    Puppies or Adult? 14

    Picking the Right Dog 15

    Locating a Reputable Breeder 18

        Questions to Ask a Reputable Breeder 19

Chapter Three: Preparing for Your Vizsla Dog 23

    Essential Tools and Supplies 23

    Puppy Proofing Your Home 25

Chapter Four: Feeding Your Vizsla Dog 29

    Vital Nutrients 29

        Protein 30

        Fat 31

        Carbohydrates 32

Water 33

Vitamins and Minerals 33

What Is a Balanced Diet? 35

Choosing Dog Food 36

Canned Food 38

Dry Food 39

Frozen and Semi-Moist Food 40

Understanding the Label 41

Homemade and Raw Diets 44

Commercial Dog Foods 45

How and When to Feed 47

Supplements 48

Treat Talk 49

Foods To Avoid 50

Obesity 52

Chapter Five: Grooming Your Vizsla Dog 53

Use a Groomer or Do It Yourself? 54

Grooming Supplies 55

Brushing and Combing 56

Removing Mats 57

Bathing 57

Bathing Essentials 58

The Dog Wash 59

Cleaning Ears 59

Clipping Toenails 60

    Handling His Feet 61

    Trimming Your Vizsla's Toenails 61

Dental Hygiene 62

    Brushing Your Vizsla's Teeth 62

    The Need for Dentist 63

    Dental Problems 64

Anal Sacs 65

Removing Skunk Odor 65

Removing Sticky Substances 66

Chapter Six: Training and Behavior Modification 69

    Obedience Training 69

        How to Teach a Dog to Sit 70

        How to Teach the Dog to Come 71

        "Lie Down" Command 72

    Train the "No" Command 74

    Train Your Dog To "Stay." 75

    Train Your Dog To "Get Off." 76

        The "Leave It" Command 77

Potty Training 77

Crate Training	80
Unwanted Behavior	82
Your Dog's Instinctive Response to Authority	82
Dog Training for Desired Behaviors	84
Your Dog's Motivation for Behaving Badly	86
Refusing to Come when Called	87
Eliminating Biting Behaviors	90
Preventing Biting and Mouthing	90
Using Trust to Prevent Biting	92
Eliminating Bad Habits	92
Whining, Howling and Excessive Barking	93
Problem Chewing	95
Jumping On People	96
Straining and Pulling at the Leash	97
Escaping and Roaming	99
Socializing	101
1. With Other Dogs and Pets	102
2. With Other People	105
3. Within Different Environments	106
4. Loud Noises	107
Chapter Seven: Vet Care for Your Vizsla Dog	111
Spaying and Neutering	112

Vaccinations 114

Performing Health Check 115

    Checking the Head 115

    Checking the Body 116

How to Take Your Dog's Temperature 117

Common Illnesses and Injuries 118

    When Do You Need to Visit the Vet? 118

    Allergies 119

    Cuts, Scrapes, and Foxtails 123

    Diarrhea, Vomiting, and Lack of Appetite 124

    Lumps and Bumps 126

    Orthopedic Problems 129

    Eye Diseases 132

    Tricuspid Valve Dysplasia (TVD) 134

    Epilepsy 134

Emergencies 135

    First-Aid Kit 135

    How to Muzzle Your Vizsla 137

    Does Your Vizsla Need CPR? 138

    How to Move an Injured Dog 141

    Dealing with Emergencies 142

Chapter Eight: Showing Your Vizsla Dog 153

    Vizsla Breed Standards 154

    What to Know Before You Show 156

    Preparing Your Dog for Show... 157

Chapter Nine: Breeding Your Vizsla Dog 159

    The Breeding Process.. 159

    Sexual Problems In Dogs 162

    Few Precautions To Take 165

    Health Factors To Consider Before Mating....................... 167

    Weaning... 169

    Food 170

Conclusion 171

Glossary of Terms 173

Index 179

Photo Credits 187

References 189

Introduction

The Vizsla is a Hungarian hunting dog known for its sleek appearance, impressive endurance, and its beautiful reddish brown coat. These dogs are the ideal sporting breed but they also make very loyal companions. Not only are Vizslas excellent hunters of fowl and upland game, but they are actually one of the smallest pointer-retriever breeds. If you are looking for a talented hunting breed that lives for sport but you do not want a giant dog around the house, the Vizsla might be a good compromise.

This hunting dog is medium-sized in terms of its build, but it packs a great deal of power and stamina into its small frame. The Vizsla is not just known for its hunting prowess but also for its outstanding trainability. This breed is incredibly intelligent and eager to learn. This is why it performs so well in a variety of dog sports including hunting, agility trials, and obedience. The Vizsla is a lively and well-mannered breed, though it does have strong protective instincts. Out in the field, the Vizsla is fearless and devoted to the hunt, but in the home, he is sensitive and affectionate with family.

Overall, the Vizsla is built for sport but it can be adaptable to a variety of living conditions. As long as the dog gets enough exercise to work off its energy, the Vizsla will be perfectly happy as a family pet. These dogs are actually one of the few sporting breeds that do very well as family pets and companion animals. Most hunting breeds prefer the company of other dogs, but the Vizsla can become very attached to his

Introduction

human companions and he generally gets on well with children.

Chapter One: Vizsla Dog Facts and Descriptions

Facts About Vizsla Dogs

Also known as the Hungarian Vizsla or the Magyar Vizsla, the Vizsla originated in Hungary. This breed belongs to the Sporting Group for the AKC and the Pointer Group (Group 7) for the Federation Cynologique Internationale (FCI). One of the most appealing characteristics of the Vizsla breed is its medium size. Many hounds and pointing breeds are much larger than the Vizsla. In addition to being medium-sized, the Vizsla is gentle and well-mannered in temperament which once again makes it a great family pet.

Chapter One: Vizsla Dog Facts and Descriptions

Vizsla dogs have short, close-lying coats that are fairly dense, but these dogs do not have a woolly undercoat. Because its coat is so short, and because the undercoat is absent, this breed is not well-suited to living outdoors. Though this dog cannot be kept outside, it is unique among indoor dogs in that it doesn't require a lot of grooming or bathing. The Vizsla is only an average shedder and it is generally a self-cleaning breed. In fact, the Vizsla does not have the characteristic "dog" smell that many people complain of in other breeds.

In addition to its medium size and hunting prowess, another identifying characteristic of the Vizsla dog breed is its rust-colored coat. The standard coat for the dog breed Vizsla is a solid golden-rust color and it may come in several different shadings. Some describe the Vizsla coat color as copper, russet gold, or dark sandy gold. The only colorations that are considered faults or a disqualification in show are the pale yellow and the solid dark mahogany colorations. Some white markings on the fore-chest, tail, and neck are allowed but not preferred. The color of the Vizsla's eyes, nose and nails usually blend with the coat.

In terms of its size, the male Vizsla stands about 22 to 25 inches (56-64 cm) tall and the average male Vizsla weight is between 45 and 66 lbs. (20 to 30 kg). The female Vizsla size is about 21 to 24 inches (53 to 61 cm) tall and weighs 40 to 55 lbs. (18 to 25 kg) at maturity. The Vizsla has a very long natural tail but the American breed standard calls for it to be docked at two-thirds the original length. Tail docking is banned in several countries so Vizslas in areas like the UK do

Chapter One: Vizsla Dog Facts and Descriptions

not have this same requirement. As the Vizsla tracks game it holds its tail perpendicular to the ground, wagging it vigorously as it runs. The Vizsla's tail is much longer than the tails of other docked breeds such as the Boxer, Weimaraner, and the Doberman. There is some variation in tail length among Vizslas because docking is usually performed at 3 days after birth.

Again, in terms of Vizsla temperament, this is usually a gentle and well-mannered breed. While many hounds and pointers prefer the company of other dogs and do not form strong bonds with their owners, the Vizsla makes an excellent family pet and companion. These dogs want to spend as much time with their owners as possible and they usually do well around children. The Vizsla thrives on exercise and human interaction which contributes to this breed's success as a household pet. Sometimes the Vizsla is nicknamed the "Velcro dog" because of their tendency to stick close to their owners.

The Vizsla has very strong protective instincts and he may be wary around strangers, particularly if he thinks they may be a threat to the family, his "pack". These dogs can be trained as guard dogs because they do not hesitate to bark at intruders on their perceived territory. This breed is also excellent at various dog sports because it is very intelligent and trainable. One thing to be wary of with this breed is that it can become whiny or develop behavior problems if it doesn't get enough attention or exercise. Vizsla puppies should begin training and socialization as early as possible,

Chapter One: Vizsla Dog Facts and Descriptions

and you should maintain a firm and consistent hand in training.

For the most part, the Vizsla is a healthy breed and it has an average lifespan between 10 and 14 years. Though the Vizsla lifespan is fairly long, there are a few heritable conditions to which the breed is prone. Vizslas are at-risk of developing hip dysplasia, canine epilepsy, lymphoma, hemangiosarcoma, and sebaceous adenitis. Responsible breeding practices can help to reduce the risk for these disease in Vizsla puppies. Having your dog seen regularly by a veterinarian and making sure he stays up to date on vaccinations will also help to ensure his health.

Summary of Vizsla Facts

- **Pedigree**: ancestors were hunting dogs of the Magyar tribes living in the Carpathian Basin during the 10th century

- **Breed Size**: medium

- **Height (male)**: 22 to 25 inches (56-64 cm)

- **Height (female)**: 21 to 24 inches (53 to 61 cm)

- **Weight (male)**: 45 to 66 lbs. (20 to 30 kg)

- **Weight (female):** 40 to 55 lbs. (18 to 25 kg)

- **Coat Length**: short and close-lying

Chapter One: Vizsla Dog Facts and Descriptions

- **Coat Texture**: smooth and dense; no woolly undercoat (obviously relatively rough coated with the wirehaired type.)

- **Color**: solid golden-rust; dark mahogany or pale yellow are considered faults

- **Markings**: some small white markings on the forehead, chest, neck, and tail are permissible

- **Eyes and Nose**: reddish; eye, nose, and nail color should blend with the coat color

- **Ears**: drop ears; very thin leather

- **Tail**: very long; usually docked at two-thirds length

- **Temperament**: high-energy, loyal, well-mannered, affectionate and intelligent.

- **Training**: intelligent and extremely trainable

- **Exercise Needs**: fairly high; long daily walk or jog recommended; breed is likely to develop problem behaviors without adequate mental/physical stimulation

- **Lifespan**: average 10 to 14 years

- **Health Conditions**: hip dysplasia, canine epilepsy, lymphoma, hemangiosarcoma, and sebaceous adenitis

Chapter One: Vizsla Dog Facts and Descriptions

Vizsla Breed History

The exact origins of the Vizsla are unknown because it is a very old breed. It is hypothesized, however, that the ancestors of the breed were native dogs used for hunting by the Magyar tribes that lived in the Carpathian Basin during the 10th century. There are primitive stone etchings dated more than a thousand years showing Magyar hunters with both his falcon and his Vizsla dog. The first written reference to the breed didn't occur until 1357. It was recorded in the *Illustrated Vienna Chronicle* by the Carmelite Friars.

For many centuries, the Vizsla was prized as a companion dog by barons and warlords. As a result, the bloodline was preserved and kept pure by the aristocracy who guarded the breed jealously. In addition to preserving the bloodline of Vizslas, the aristocracy also helped to develop the breed's hunting abilities. The popularity of the breed helped it to survive the Turkish occupation lasting from 1526 to 1696 and the Hungarian Revolution between 1848 and 1849. The breed stayed strong through two World Wars and the Soviet Period.

During the 1800s and early 1900s however, the breed faced several near-extinctions. After World War II, breed fanciers sought out Vizslas of the true type and used them to revive the breed. At the close of World War II, the Vizsla was brought to the United States for the first time. Here, its popularity continued to rise and the Vizsla Club of America was formed in the 1950s. The Vizsla remains one of the top 50 breeds in the UK with about 1,000 puppies being registered

Chapter One: Vizsla Dog Facts and Descriptions

with the Kennel Club each year. A Vizsla even won Best-in-Show at the 2010 Crufts show.

Chapter One: Vizsla Dog Facts and Descriptions

Chapter Two: Choosing and Acquiring a Vizsla Dog

Where to Look For Vizsla Dogs?

Breeders

If you are interested in adopting your new Vizsla from a breeder, it is important to remember that not all breeders are created equal. Some establishments that may call themselves breeders are actually puppy mills, large scale breeding operations solely concerned with turning a profit. You may also be looking at an unlicensed breeder who is, in reality, just a random person who happens to have a dog with papers and wants to make money. In either case, making money is prioritized over the well being of the animal, often resulting in puppies that are in poor health.

So how do you avoid getting your new dog from one of these so-called breeders? Remember that they are overly concerned with profit. The breeder that you want to deal with is the breeder that respects the process and cares about the health of the animals being produced. These types of breeders will not simply hand puppies out to anyone who comes along. They will want to make sure that you are someone who is equipped to properly manage and care for the animal.

You should also Breed and Kennel Clubs as they can be excellent resources for finding a responsible dog breeder.

Once you've found a possible puppy, ask to see where the puppies spend their time and keep an eye on the cleanliness of the location. Examine the dogs themselves to check for health concerns or general lethargy. Remember that a happy and healthy puppy is usually also a lively one. Ask for vet records and information on care and training. A good breeder should also be a knowledgeable one. Finally, make sure there is a contract. A formal contract is a sign of professionalism.

One last thing to note when looking at breeders is the number of breeds being represented. Puppy mills tend to be indiscriminate about how many breeds they churn out. If you are looking for a healthy Vizsla from a trusted breeder, look for breeders that deal solely in Vizsla dogs. This will be the first step in finding a trustworthy organization.

Chapter Two: Choosing and Acquiring a Vizsla Dog

do you start looking for a Vizsla breeder? Breeders for various breeds of dog are located all over the country. A simple Google search could help you find one that is conveniently located to you. The American Kennel Club can also help you locate approved breeders through their website. Any breeders found here would be members of an AKC licensed club or part of member clubs that have AKC registerable puppies available.

Rescues

If you are worried about buying from the right kind of breeder or the expense of buying from a breeder is more than you can manage at the moment, you can also try looking at Vizsla rescues for dogs in desperate need of a good home.

Right now there are dozens of Vizsla rescues all over the country. A quick Google search could yield a variety of lists that provide links to every rescue. In fact, nearly every single state can boast a rescue or two for Vizsla dogs. Several, New York and Florida among them, can boast more than four individual rescues.

Just as with breeders, you want to make sure that you are dealing with a reputable organization before you make your move to adopt a new pet. First and foremost, rescues are nonprofits and should be registered charities. They should also be well staffed and responsive. Organizations that can't take care of or retain employees may have similar challenges when properly taking the needs of a rescue dog into consideration. Don't be afraid to ask questions and even visit the facility in person before deciding to adopt a dog through them. You should also not be shy about doing a little research on the organization. Check out reviews and any other indications of what the public perception of the rescue might be.

Let's say that you've done your research and you've found the perfect place with the perfect dog. Be prepared for the third degree. Remember that adopting from a rescue is not the same as adopting from a shelter. These are not simply dogs that people decided they were no longer equipped to care for. Rescue dogs may have suffered neglect, abandonment, or abuse. Rescues will have worked hard to rehabilitate these animals and they want to make sure that their new homes will be improvements upon their old ones. This may seem frustrating when all you want to do is play with your new best friend, but try to remember that it is in everyone's best interest including the Vizsla that you will soon come to love.

Puppies or Adult?

Whether or not to buy a puppy is a serious question. Now that we've taken some time to go over where to find and what you can expect from breeders and rescues, it's time to think about which is a better choice for you. If you find yourself desperate to start playing with Tiny Fido in the backyard, then you're probably eager to get your hands on a

Chapter Two: Choosing and Acquiring a Vizsla Dog

Vizsla puppy. Puppies can be a wonderful choice and not just for the obvious reasons.

It's already been stated that a puppy is more impressionable than an adult Vizsla. If you have some experience with training and you want to nurture your dog from the ground up, making sure both your furniture and your sanity stay in one piece, puppies may be the way to go. It makes for a more subtle transition into the Vizsla experience, avoiding a situation where you suddenly go from no dog to 120 lbs. of black and tan beast.

However, consider the possibility of giving that adult rescue with the curious black eyes and untamed saliva a chance. Adult dogs can actually be easier to handle than their wriggly counterparts. True, it may be harder to teach them "new tricks" as the adage goes, but you don't need new tricks when the old ones work just as well. Many of these dogs may already be socialized for animals and children, making your life substantially easier. Their personalities are already established, allowing you to know exactly what kind of fit they are instead of hoping and praying that Tiny Fido doesn't grow up to redecorate your living room.

Picking the Right Dog

Whether you decide to go with a puppy or a fully-grown Vizsla, there a few items to consider before picking out your new best friend. First and foremost, you need to remember that this is not a question of good or bad dogs, nor

Chapter Two: Choosing and Acquiring a Vizsla Dog

is it a question of good or bad families. This is simply a matter of comparing the particular needs of the dog with the particular needs of the family and finding the right match.

Before even considering Vizsla dogs as a breed, assess how much space you have for the dog to move around. Also look to your activity level and that of the other members of your household. Are you equipped to handle an energetic dog of the Vizsla's size? Are you able to keep up with this breed and provide them with the attention they require? You will also want to evaluate the financial burden of owning a dog. Vizsla dogs can be terrific companions, but all dogs require equipment, food, and the occasional visit to the vet. Additionally, Vizsla dogs may benefit from classes to help train and socialize them. Finally, ask yourself if you are truly committed to owning a dog. It benefits neither the dog nor you to make a rash decision. While it is true that no one can know what they're life will look like in the future and what obstacles life might conjure up, you should still ask yourself if you can imagine this pet with your family in ten or twelve years. Remember that dogs are sensitive and loving animals that will depend on you.

Let's say you've fully analyzed your dog owning capabilities and have decided that you are equipped to handle the Vizsla you've been longing to have. When considering a fully-grown rescue dog, ask yourself a few extra questions about your own situation before looking at the available adoptees. Do you have any other pets or children in the home? Do you frequently have visitors that may bring pets or children with them? Are you looking for a dog that you can

Chapter Two: Choosing and Acquiring a Vizsla Dog

take on trips with you or a dog that would otherwise be spending a decent amount of time in a car? Is your neighborhood a crowded one? Are there a lot of loud noises? These may seem like arbitrary questions, but they can make a huge difference when considering the unique temperaments of rescue dogs. Remember that these dogs have developed personalities at this stage and many will have already decided things about cats, children, cars, and noises that can't easily be altered. Ask the rescue about these temperaments and get to know each of the available Vizsla dogs.

If you find one that matches your particular needs and situation, take advantage of a trial period if offered by the rescue. Many rescues will allow families to take dogs home for several days in order to confirm that the match is a good one. Ask about this option. Finally, once the trial period is over, be honest with yourself about how it went. If it was a success, then congratulations. You have a new family member. If not, don't feel bad. As previously stated, it is in everyone's best interest that you find the right dog. You are not letting the dog down if you return him to the rescue; you are helping him find the right family too.

Getting a Vizsla puppy is comparatively simple. The most important thing to note is just that you should make sure to consider not only the needs of the puppy, but also the needs of the adult Vizsla the puppy will one day become. Puppies may seem cuddly, lovable, and easy. However, they do need the proper training and attention. Not to mention, they can be extremely high energy. Making sure you can manage these behaviors is essential to owning any puppy, especially a tiny

Chapter Two: Choosing and Acquiring a Vizsla Dog

Vizsla. Assuming you've considered this aspect of owning a puppy and are ready to move forward, there are some additional considerations to be taken into account.

Puppies, like people, come down to a combination of nature and nurture. In other words, training and socialization can help, but a puppy's predispositions may also influence what type of adult it will become. When choosing a puppy from a breeder, ask to see the parents. Check that they are healthy looking and even-tempered. Don't be afraid to ask how many times the mother has been bred either. The more a dog has been bred, the more likely it is that she will produce puppies with health issues. Again, make sure that the breeder is reputable. Check that the puppy is healthy, well fed, and has a certificate of health.

Finding the right dog is no easy task, nor should it be. This is a big decision for any individual or family and should be taken very seriously. That being said, once you've done the work and have brought home a new friend that you know will be a good fit for your lifestyle, you will not be disappointed. A Vizsla can and will make a loyal and heartwarming long-time companion.

Locating a Reputable Breeder

You now know things to look out for when searching for a Vizsla. You're searching for a breeder who will screen for genetic diseases, be choosy about which dogs she breeds so that she produces the very best, and will guarantee her

Chapter Two: Choosing and Acquiring a Vizsla Dog

dogs–that is, will replace or refund the price of the dog if a genetic health problem occurs and will take back a dog under any circumstance.

Questions to Ask a Reputable Breeder

But where do you find such a breeder? As you may guess, you're not likely to find them in classified ads, although occasionally you might. Contact the American Vizsla Club for a referral list of those breeders in your area.

But your job isn't done yet. Contact a few breeders in your area and ask if they're planning on breeding a litter any time soon. You should then ask questions to determine if the breeder is a responsible or reputable breeder.

1. How long have you been interested in Vizsla dogs?
2. How long have you been breeding Vizsla dogs?
3. Do you show (or participate in performance events with) your Vizsla dogs? Are you affiliated with any local or national clubs?
4. What titles do your dogs have? With what organizations?
5. Why did you choose to breed these two Vizsla dogs? Do you breed for show, work, or performance?

Chapter Two: Choosing and Acquiring a Vizsla Dog

6. What can you tell me about their ancestry and what makes them suitable to breed?
7. How many litters do you produce each year?
8. Do you screen for genetic diseases? Which ones? Can you show me the original certificates?
9. Are your dogs AKC registered? Can you show me the papers?
10. Do you have a contract? May I see the contract? Do you offer guarantees for hips, eyes, etc.?
11. May I have a tour of your kennel and meet you and your dogs?
12. Can you provide references?

If the breeder isn't put off by your questions and is willing to answer, you may have found a reputable breeder. Reputable breeders like talking to informed puppy buyers and will be happy to answer any of your questions. If the breeder on the other end of the line acts affronted, look for your puppy somewhere else!

When you visit a reputable breeder, you should be able to meet with any of the dogs there (with a proper introduction). The kennels should be well maintained, and you should feel comfortable meeting with the dogs and the breeder. Keep in mind, though, that if there are puppies, it is natural for the female Vizsla to be protective of them.

Chapter Two: Choosing and Acquiring a Vizsla Dog

A reputable breeder will not pressure you into buying a puppy right there. The breeder may want to meet your entire family to see how they react to Vizsla dogs. Don't forget, these are big dogs and require a certain amount of responsibility.

Chapter Two: Choosing and Acquiring a Vizsla Dog

Chapter Three: Preparing for Your Vizsla Dog

Essential Tools and Supplies

Before bringing home your new puppy or dog for the first time, there will be a list of items you need to make sure you have on hand, including:

- **Food** – usually the puppy will remain on whatever food they have been fed at the breeder's for at least the first couple of weeks, until they are well settled in their new home, so make sure you ask the breeder what brand to buy.

Chapter Three: Preparing for Your Vizsla Dog

- **Food and Water Bowls** – make sure they are small enough for a young puppy to get close to so that they can easily eat and drink.
- **Kennel** – when you buy your puppy's hard-sided kennel, make sure that you buy the size that will be appropriate for them when they are fully grown. It must be large enough so that (when fully grown) they can easily stand up and turn around inside it.
- **Martingale Collar, 2 Leashes and Harness** – buy the harness and collar small enough to fit your puppy and buy new collars as they grow larger.
- **Leashes** – you will be able to keep the same leashes as all you will ever need is a four foot (1.22 meters) leash made out of nylon webbing with a light weight clip at the end (do not buy a leash that has a heavy clip on the end as it will be difficult for your puppy to carry around).
- **Soft Beds** – you will need one or two for comfortable sleeping when they are not in their kennel. Make sure that you buy the beds large enough for a full-grown dog.
- **Canine Shampoo and Conditioner** – always choose products that are the correct pH for a dog (never use human products). You will also need a non-slip mat for the sink or bathtub and lots of drying towels.

Chapter Three: Preparing for Your Vizsla Dog

- **Finger Tooth Brush** –- this is a soft, rubber cap that fits over the human's finger to get the puppy used to having their teeth regularly brushed, then a regular or electric toothbrush (an Oral-B electric is best).
- **Soft Bristle Brush or Comb**– for daily grooming.
- **Puppy Nail Scissors** – for trimming their toenails, and a small, medium or large-sized pair of plier style nail clippers for when they are full grown.
- **One or two Soft Toys** – or wait until they come home and let them pick their own toys from the store.
- **Daily Essentials – Pee Pads, Puppy sized Treats, Poop Bags.** Be sure to take your shopping list with you when you go to your local pet store or boutique, otherwise you may forget critical items.

NOTE: if you do not already have a hairdryer, you will need to get one of these, too, so you can dry your puppy after bath time.

Puppy Proofing Your Home

Most puppies will be a curious bundle of energy, eager to explore everything, which means that they will get into everything within their reach.

Chapter Three: Preparing for Your Vizsla Dog

As a responsible puppy guardian, you will want to provide a safe environment for them, which means eliminating all sources of danger, similar to what you would do for a curious toddler.

Be aware that your puppy will want to touch, sniff, taste, chew, investigate and closely inspect every electrical cord, every closet, every nook and cranny of your home and everything you may have left lying about on the floor.

Power cords can be found in just about every room in the home and to a teething puppy, these may look like irresistible, fun chew toys. Make sure that you tuck all power cords securely out of your puppy's reach or enclose them inside a chew-proof PVC tube.

Kitchen – first of all, there are many human foods that can be harmful to dogs, therefore, your kitchen should always be strictly off limits to your puppy any time you are preparing food. Calmly send them out of the kitchen any time you are in the kitchen, and they will quickly get the idea that this area is off limits to them.

Bathroom – bathroom cupboards and drawers or the side of a bathtub where you may leave your shaving supplies can hold many dangers for a young and curious puppy. Kleenex, cotton swabs, Q-tips, toilet paper, razors, pills, soap or other materials left within your puppy's reach are an easy target that could result in an emergency visit to your veterinarian's office. Family members need to put shampoos, soap, facial products, makeup and accessories out of reach or safely inside a cabinet or drawer.

Chapter Three: Preparing for Your Vizsla Dog

Bedroom – if you don't keep your shoes, slippers and clothing safely behind doors, you may find that your puppy has claimed them for their new chew toys. Be vigilant about keeping everything in its safe place, including jewelry, hair ties, bills, coins, and other items small enough for them to swallow in containers or drawers, and secure any exposed cords or wires.

If you have children, make sure they understand that, especially while your puppy is going through their teething stage, they must keep their rooms picked up and leave nothing that could cause a choking problem to the puppy lying about on the floor or within their reach.

Living Room – we humans spend many hours in our cozy gathering places to watch movies or play games, and often the living areas of our homes will have many items that are very enticing for a curious and teething puppy, such as books, magazines, pillows, iPods, cell phones, TV remotes and more.

You will want to keep your home free of excess clutter and remain vigilant about straightening up and putting things out of sight that could be tempting to your puppy.

Office – we often spend a great deal of time in our home offices, which means that our puppy will want to be there, too, and they will be curious about all the items an office has to offer, such as cell phones, papers, books, magazines, and electrical cords.

Chapter Three: Preparing for Your Vizsla Dog

Although your puppy might think that rubber bands or paper clips are fun to play with, allowing these items to be within your puppy's reach could end up being a fatal mistake if your puppy swallows them.

Plants: – can be a very tempting target for your puppy's teeth, so you will want to keep them well out their reach. If you have floor plants, they will need to be moved to a shelf or counter or placed behind a closed door until your curious fur friend grows out of the habit of putting everything in their mouth. Also keep in mind that many common houseplants are poisonous to dogs.

Garage and Yard – there are obvious as well as subtle dangers that could seriously harm or even kill a puppy, which can often be found in the garage or yard. Some of these might include antifreeze, gasoline, fertilizers, rat, mice, snail and slug poison, weed killer, paint, cleaners and solvents, grass seed, bark mulch and various insecticides.

If you are storing any of these toxic substances in your garage or garden shed, make certain that you keep all such products inside a locked cabinet, or stored on high shelves that your puppy will not be able to reach. Even better, choose not to use toxic chemicals anywhere in your home or yard.

Chapter Four: Feeding Your Vizsla Dog

The quality of dog foods available ranges from barely-qualifies-as-food to good-enough-to-eat-myself. To figure out which food is best for your Vizsla, it helps to know some nutrition basics.

Vital Nutrients

Nutrients are substances that provide energy, promote growth, and help the body perform metabolic functions, such as regulating temperature, maintaining and synthesizing tissues. The nutrients a dog needs to maintain life and health are protein, carbohydrates, fats, vitamins, minerals, and

Chapter Four: Feeding Your Vizsla Dog

water. These nutrients are found in meats, grains, fruits, and vegetables. A balanced diet supplies all the nutrients a dog needs.

Protein

Proteins are the building blocks of enzymes and hormones. The body uses proteins to create protective and structural tissues, such as skin, hair, nails, cartilage, ligaments, and tendons. Proteins carry oxygen and iron to the tissues and form the antibodies the immune system uses to fight disease.

The units that make up proteins are called amino acids. They are important in tissue growth and repair. Without amino acids, your Vizsla's body couldn't function. These multifunctional units can be used directly for energy or stored as fat or glycogen for later use as energy.

Providing high-quality nutrients in the correct amounts is one of the best ways to ensure that a puppy leads a long and healthy life. Each nutrient plays a pivotal role in the way the body functions.

Sources of protein are meat, grains, or a combination of the two. Common meat proteins you might see listed on a dog food label are beef, chicken meal, and meat by-products. The quality of animal protein varies, ranging from poor to excellent. For instance, the protein quality of chicken depends on whether the food contains chicken meat and skin, or chicken feathers, bones, heads, and feet. Bones and feathers are made up of collagen, a protein that isn't easily digested, so they aren't a good source of protein.

Fat

Fats, also known as lipids, provide energy and make food taste good. Fat pads vital organs, protecting them from injury, and serves as insulation, helping the body conserve heat. Among other things, the body uses fats to help transmit nerve impulses and transport nutrients. The essential fatty acids in fats contain the fat-soluble vitamins A, D, E, and K. All are essential for a number of bodily functions, such as gastric acid secretion, inflammation control, and muscle contraction.

Animal fats and vegetable oils are the sources of fat in dog foods. If a single type of fat is used in a food — chicken fat, for example — it must be described that way on the ingredient label. Otherwise, you'll see the general term "animal fat."

Besides providing the most concentrated form of energy of all the nutrients, fat is also highly digestible. Despite these advantages, high-fat foods taste so good that dogs — especially Vizslas — are likely to eat too much of them. That's why it's important to use portion control.

Carbohydrates

Carbohydrates are a plant-based source of energy that fuel the Vizsla to run and retrieve for hours on end. When it needs energy, the body uses carbs first so that protein can be spared for other uses, such as tissue repair and growth. In addition to serving as an energy source, carbohydrates help form the nonessential amino acids produced by the dog's body. When joined with proteins or fats, carbs play a role in the construction of body tissues. Without carbohydrates, the body couldn't synthesize DNA, RNA, or other essential body compounds.

Carbohydrates can take three forms: simple sugars, such as glucose; complex sugars, such as lactose and sucrose; and polysaccharides, such as glycogen and dietary fiber. Sugars provide energy for tissues and are essential to the functioning of the central nervous system. Glycogen, which is stored in muscle and the liver, provides emergency energy for the heart and cells. Fiber helps stimulate bowel movements and speeds waste through the system.

Grains, such as corn, oats, rice, and wheat are the primary sources of carbohydrates in dog foods. They provide the body with complex carbohydrates in the form of starch. Other plant sources, such as beet pulp and rice or wheat bran, provide fiber.

Chapter Four: Feeding Your Vizsla Dog

Water

Although we may not think of it as such, water is the most important nutrient in a dog's diet. Water, which comprises almost 60 percent of an adult dog's body and 75 to 80 percent of a puppy's body, plays a vital role in cell and organ function. It helps maintain body temperature, aids in digestion and circulation, transports nutrients, lubricates body tissues, and facilitates elimination of waste. Dogs can go for weeks without food, but without water they can die within days.

A number of factors control water intake: thirst, hunger, metabolic activity (such as growth or pregnancy), and environmental conditions (such as temperature and humidity). The amount of water your Vizsla drinks and loses each day varies depending on the amount of food he eats. That's why it's important to make sure he has an ample supply of fresh water every day. Dogs that eat canned food, which is about 75 percent water, tend to drink less water than dogs that eat kibble (dry food).

Vitamins and Minerals

In minute amounts, these organic molecules serve a vital function in many of the body's metabolic processes. Vitamins are classified in two groups: fat-soluble and water-soluble. Fat-soluble vitamins — A, D, E, and K — can be stored in the liver, while water-soluble vitamins are excreted in the urine if the body doesn't use them. Among the vitamins you might see listed on a dog-food label are thiamin, riboflavin, niacin, pyridoxine, panthothenic acid, biotin, folic acid, and choline.

With a few exceptions, most vitamins can't be synthesized by the body and must be supplied in a dog's food. Vitamin C is one of those exceptions. Dogs can synthesize the necessary levels of vitamin C, so they don't need it added to their diet.

Because fat-soluble vitamins are stored primarily in the liver, they can quickly reach toxic levels if dogs are supplemented with them too frequently.

Like vitamins, minerals are present in your Vizsla's body only in tiny amounts, but they too are essential for life. Among other functions, minerals provide skeletal support and play a role in nerve transmission and muscle contractions. Macrominerals, which include calcium, phosphorus, and magnesium, account for most of the body's mineral content. Microminerals, also called trace elements, are present in the body in very small amounts. Microminerals include zinc, manganese, iodine, and selenium.

Proper vitamin and mineral balance is essential, but that doesn't mean you should automatically supplement your Vizsla's diet. Especially during puppyhood, an overdose of certain vitamins and minerals can cause problems in musculoskeletal development. The level of vitamins and minerals in a dog food should be considered in relation to other components of the diet. The goal is an overall balanced diet.

Chapter Four: Feeding Your Vizsla Dog

What Is a Balanced Diet?

For sparkling good health, every Vizsla needs an appropriate mix of protein, fat, carbohydrates, vitamins, and minerals. A balanced diet contains all the nutrients that dogs are known to need. Nutritional requirements are usually determined as the amount of a given nutrient a dog needs to support growth or to fulfill a needed function.

When dogs don't get enough of a particular essential nutrient, they can develop problems related to that nutrient's functions. For instance, the body uses protein to synthesize new protein, as well as for energy. If the amount of fat and carbohydrate in a diet are not balanced to the amount of protein, then the protein ends up being used for energy instead of for synthesis of new protein. The result is protein malnutrition.

The statement that a diet is complete and balanced has meaning on two levels. Complete means that a food contains all the nutrients that dogs are known to need. Balanced means that a food contains those nutrients in appropriate proportions to one another and also that those nutrients are balanced to the energy level of the diet. For instance, a diet formulated for older dogs is balanced to provide a lower energy level than one formulated for puppies.

Is there a balanced diet that's right for every dog?

No, there is no set balanced diet that's right for every dog. Dogs are individuals, and while a majority of them might do quite well on a given diet, there will always be a few that have special needs. A dog's dietary needs can also be affected by stress, environment, and other factors.

To determine whether a particular food is complete and balanced, look on the label. Manufacturers must state whether their foods meet the nutrient profiles set by a group called the American Association of Feed Control Officials (AAFCO). Growth diets (puppy food) and maintenance diets (adult food) have different nutrient profiles. Some foods are labeled for "all life stages," but for a puppy, a food labeled for growth is a better choice.

Beyond that, look to see whether the food is formulated to meet AAFCO standards or whether the manufacturer conducted feeding trials to see if dogs actually thrive on the diet. Look for a nutritional adequacy statement that says something like "This food is complete and balanced for maintenance [or for growth] based on AAFCO feeding trials." When in doubt, go with a food that's backed by feeding tests.

Choosing Dog Food

When you stroll down the numerous dog food aisles at your pet supply store, you may be overwhelmed by the variety available. You can find foods for puppies, medium-breed puppies, old dogs, working dogs, and dogs with allergies. While it's nice to have a selection, it can be difficult to decide which food is right for your dog. Knowing the Vizsla's special needs will help.

Chapter Four: Feeding Your Vizsla Dog

Factors to consider include the dog's energy level and size. Working dogs, or active, high-energy dogs, such as Vizslas, are probably better off with a diet that's high in caloric density, meaning that it's high in fat and highly digestible. Couch potatoes, on the other hand, who get most of their exercise walking to and from the food bowl, need a much lower calorie diet or they'll become overweight.

With a puppy, you need to be aware of growth rate. Conventional wisdom once said that big dogs with big bones needed lots of calcium and other nutrients during puppyhood. Veterinarians now know that's not true. Because Vizslas are prone to musculoskeletal disorders, such as hip and elbow dysplasia, it's important that they not grow too quickly.

Medium-breed puppies, such as Vizslas, need less calcium so their bones can develop normally as they're growing. Veterinary nutrition researchers have discovered that by reducing the calcium in diets for medium-breed puppies and controlling the calories, the puppies don't grow as quickly and grow up with fewer musculoskeletal problems. Some manufacturers also add nutrients believed to help improve joint cartilage — such as glucosamine and chondroitin — to the foods for medium-breed puppies, as well as to diets for medium-breed adult dogs.

Keep in mind that a regular puppy food, as opposed to one that's made specifically for medium-breed puppies, provides complete and balanced nutrition for any size dog. The difference is that it's not fine-tuned to meet the precise needs of a puppy that will grow up to be a big dog, such as a

Vizsla. Medium-breed dogs are defined as those that will weigh 50 pounds or more in adulthood. Most dogs, such as Vizslas, that will weigh less than 90 pounds at maturity can be switched to an adult diet at about one year of age. Whatever you choose to feed your puppy, the most important thing is for it to be complete and balanced. As a puppy grows, poor nutrition can lead to all sorts of problems, from poor skeletal development to a compromised immune system.

Canned Food

Canned foods contain either blends of ingredients — muscle meats or poultry, grains, vitamins, and minerals — or one/two types of muscle meats or animal by-products with enough supplemental vitamins and minerals to ensure that the food is nutritionally complete. Depending on the ingredients used, canned foods can vary widely in nutrient content, digestibility, and availability of nutrients. They're prepared by cooking and blending all of the ingredients, canning and cooking the mixture, and pressure-sterilizing the sealed can.

Dogs love canned food. It meets their "smells good, tastes good" criteria. That's because canned food has a high fat content and is calorically dense. Canned food has a long shelf life, although it must be refrigerated after it's opened. It's easier to eat for older dogs that have difficulty chewing. And for you, it's easy enough to open a can and dump the contents into your Vizsla's dish.

Chapter Four: Feeding Your Vizsla Dog

However, canned food does have disadvantages. It's expensive, especially if you're feeding it to a medium breed, such as a Vizsla. Its water content is high — as much as 78 percent — so you're not getting a lot of meat for your money. Canned food sticks to teeth and is a factor in the formation of plaque, which leads to periodontal disease.

Dry Food

This is the most common type of dog food purchased. Kibble contains grains; meat, poultry, or fish; some milk products; and vitamin and mineral supplements. It's made by combining all the ingredients, extruding them into the desired shapes or sizes, and baking. Once the dog food has cooled, the kibble is sprayed with fat or some other substance to make it taste good.

The big advantage to dry food is cost. It's much less expensive than canned food. This is something to consider when you have one or more medium dogs to feed. Dry food has a long shelf life and can be left out without risk of going bad.

Dry food has a reputation for helping to prevent the buildup of plaque and tartar on teeth. Dry foods and biscuits can help crack off tartar (the hardened form of plaque), but they don't affect the gumline area. The exception to this is veterinary foods that are designed to have a cross-hatch effect on teeth, scrubbing them all the way to the gumline.

On the downside, kibble generally contains less fat and more carbohydrates than canned food. For this reason, it's often less palatable to dogs than canned food, especially if they're given a choice. A finicky Vizsla's taste buds can be tempted by mixing a little canned food in with the kibble.

Frozen and Semi-Moist Food

Frozen dog foods are made with fresh meat, vegetables, and fruit, and contain no artificial preservatives. After being mixed and formed into loaves, rolls, or cubes, the food is flash frozen to preserve freshness. Frozen nuggets are as easy to feed as kibble, and loaves or rolls are easy to slice after defrosting. Consider a commercial frozen food if you like the idea of fresh ingredients but don't have time to cook for the dog yourself.

The downside is that frozen dog food is available only in limited distribution. It must be kept frozen until you're ready to use it, and any unused portion must be refrigerated. If you're traveling with a dog, it's difficult to take the food along unless you have some means of refrigeration or of finding it in pet stores along the way. Some frozen foods also come in freeze-dried form and can be reconstituted with hot water. Some dogs will eat this, while others turn up their noses.

There's no evidence showing that dogs do better on one type of food than another. The choice you make depends on your Vizsla's dietary needs and preferences, as well as your preferences and budget.

The semi-moist food diet is softer than dry food but not as messy as canned food. The amount of water it contains ranges from 15 to 30 percent. Ingredients include fresh or frozen animal tissues, grains, fats, and sugars.

Other than convenience and palatability, there's not much to be said for semi-moist foods. The level of sugar they contain puts them squarely in the junk food category. In cost, they fall somewhere between canned and dry food, although single-serve packets usually compare in price to canned foods. This type of food is best given in small quantities as a treat.

Understanding the Label

Knowing how to read a dog-food label is a must if you want to choose the best food for your Vizsla. Important parts of the label that you already know about are the statement of nutritional adequacy — "complete and balanced for growth" or "complete and balanced for all life stages" — and the claim that a food's nutritional value has been proven with AAFCO feeding studies. The next thing to study is the ingredient list.

What's in It?

The label must list ingredients by weight in decreasing order. In other words, the first ingredient — which ideally is

Chapter Four: Feeding Your Vizsla Dog

some form of animal protein — cannot be exceeded in weight by any of the ingredients that come after it.

Be aware that manufacturers can get around this requirement by a practice called split-ingredient labeling. This involves spreading out, or splitting, ingredients of the same type so they appear farther down the label. For instance, a grain such as corn, rice, or wheat might appear on the label in several different forms, such as flour, flakes, middlings, or bran. A food labeled in this way might end up containing more protein from plant sources than from animal sources.

When you find a food you like, continue to check the label every once in a while to make sure the ingredients remain the same. The best dog food manufacturers use a fixed formula — meaning that the ingredients don't change from batch to batch — but others change ingredients based on availability and market prices. Some dogs with sensitive stomachs can suffer digestive upsets from this kind of unexpected change in ingredients.

You might see certain dog foods described as "premium." These are usually expensive foods that you find only in pet supply stores. The difference between premium and nonpremium foods is density per volume — in other words, a cup of a premium food generally has more usable nutrients than a cup of nonpremium food.

Name Calling

Can you tell anything from a food's name? Surprisingly, yes. There are strict regulations concerning

Chapter Four: Feeding Your Vizsla Dog

what a food can be called. Let's say that you're looking at a can that reads "Grandma's Chicken for Canines." That food must contain 95 percent chicken, not counting the water used for processing. Once the water is accounted for, the food must still contain at least 70 percent chicken. If the name includes a combination of ingredients — "Grandma's Chicken and Beef for Canines" — chicken and beef must make up 95 percent of the total weight (excluding water), and the food must contain more chicken than beef.

A food name that contains a qualifier such as "dinner," "entrée," "formula," "nuggets," or "platter" must contain at least 25 percent of the named ingredient — lamb, let's say. So "Grandma's Lamb Dinner for Dogs" contains at least 25 percent, but less than 95 percent lamb. What if Grandma makes a lamb-and-beef dinner? The lamb and beef together must make up 25 percent of the product, with at least 3 percent being beef.

Sometimes you'll see a food that highlights a special ingredient, such as bacon or cheese. Manufacturers can list these tasty ingredients if they make up at least 3 percent of the food. If you see Grandma's Beef Dinner for Dogs "with cheese," you know that it contains at least 3 percent cheese. If it says "with cheese and bacon," it must contain at least 3 percent of each ingredient.

Guaranteed Analysis

What else can you learn from the label? Look for the guaranteed analysis. This states the minimum percentages of crude protein and fat and maximum percentages of crude fiber and moisture. Sometimes it includes guarantees for other nutrients, such as calcium, phosphorus, sodium, and linoleic acid.

Because canned food has more moisture than dry food, you'll see differences between the two in the levels of crude protein and most other nutrients. To compare nutrient levels between canned and dry food, multiply the guarantees for the canned food by four. For example, if you're looking at a canned food with a guaranteed analysis of 8 percent protein, and a dry food with a guaranteed analysis of 21 percent protein, you would multiply that 8 percent by four to come up with a dry-matter percentage of 32 percent protein for the canned food.

The label also lists feeding guidelines, which are only a rough estimate. Each Vizsla is different, so you'll need to experiment to find the right amount of food for your dog. If he starts looking chubby, cut down. If he looks too thin, add more. Remember that a growing Vizsla or one that works hard in the field all day needs more food than one that lies around the house while you're at work.

Homemade and Raw Diets

The trend toward healthy eating has reached dogdom now, with more pet caregivers showing an interest in preparing a homemade or raw diet for their animals. The attraction of this type of diet is that you can control the quality of the ingredients. A homemade diet can be beneficial if your

Chapter Four: Feeding Your Vizsla Dog

Vizsla has food allergies, is sensitive to artificial dyes or preservatives, or has a particular health problem that can be benefited by a special diet.

Proponents of raw diets argue that they are more natural and provide better nutrition. Raw foods retain enzymes and other healthful substances that cooking destroys. People who feed raw diets say their dogs have better health, a beautiful coat, few or no skin problems, and great dental health. Factors to consider before deciding to feed a homemade or raw diet include nutritional completeness, time, and expense.

One of the concerns about homemade diets is that they may lack certain vitamins and minerals, or contain an improper balance of protein, fats, and carbohydrates. Simply feeding human-grade products doesn't make a diet complete and balanced. If ingredients aren't provided in proper proportions, the diet may be inadequate. It's possible to design a nutritionally complete homemade diet for dogs, but it's important to use appropriate recipes from valid sources. Look for a book by a veterinary nutritionist or a layperson trained in nutrition. It's a good idea to rotate the meats, vegetables, and fruits you use so that your Vizsla receives a variety of nutrients and stays interested in his meals.

Commercial Dog Foods

Commercial dog foods come ready to go in bags or cans. They're easy to measure out and feed. For a homemade diet, ingredients must be purchased, measured, mixed, and cooked (unless you're feeding a raw diet) on a frequent basis.

Chapter Four: Feeding Your Vizsla Dog

If you enjoy cooking and have plenty of time to spend in the kitchen, this isn't a drawback.

What if you can barely get dinner on the table for your family, let alone for the dog, but you're not satisfied with the diets you find in the grocery store? You may want to consider purchasing a natural or raw diet from a pet supply store or through mail order. Many companies produce so-called natural foods that are preservative-free and contain high-quality organic ingredients. They come in dry, canned, or raw form.

Performance Diets

Working and show dogs lead stressful lives that call for extra nutrition. They need a diet that's high in caloric density, which means that a food is high in fat to provide energy and highly digestible so the dog's body can make use of it.

This type of food is called a performance diet. It's a good choice for a Vizsla that competes in field trials, conformation shows, agility, or some other active sport. Vizslas that get lots of strenuous daily exercise, such as several long walks or hikes, can also benefit from a performance food.

Every Vizsla is different, so don't be afraid to experiment until you find a food that suits your dog, with just the right mix of nutrients. How can you tell if your Vizsla's diet is balanced for his individual needs? Simply take a look. A dog eating a well-balanced diet is bright-eyed, muscular,

Chapter Four: Feeding Your Vizsla Dog

and active, with good breath, a shiny coat, and healthy skin. Feeding a dog a balanced diet is all about choices. There's nothing wrong with feeding a commercial food if your dog is happy and healthy on it. It's convenient to feed, and it obviously meets your dog's nutritional needs. If your dog has health problems, allergies, or you'd simply like to have more control over what goes into his body, then you may want to consider some form of homemade diet. Whichever type of diet you choose, the most important thing is to make sure that it provides all the nutrients your dog needs.

How and When to Feed

How often should you feed your Vizsla puppy for optimal growth? That depends on his age. Most puppies start with four meals a day after they're weaned. By the time they're ten to twelve weeks old, they're down to three meals a day. At four months, they can start eating twice a day — a schedule that should be continued for the rest of the dog's life.

How much does a Vizsla eat?

That depends on the individual dog. Ask the breeder how much he's been feeding at each meal, and go from there. You can also use the recommendation on the food's label as a starting point, but remember that it's only an estimate — it may be too much or too little for your particular Vizsla.

If you're a working caregiver, though, it's not always convenient to fit in that third or fourth meal. When that's the case, it's perfectly fine to feed puppies only twice a day — morning and evening. It won't make any difference in their activity level or behavior. Just divide the amount of food they need daily into two meals instead of three or four.

As with housetraining, a routine is important. Try to feed your Vizsla at the same time every day. Feeding meals at set times rather than leaving food out all the time allows you to be aware of how much your dog is eating and whether his appetite is good. And free-feeding (leaving food out all the time) promotes obesity, which can be a problem in this breed.

Supplements

One aspect of feeding a balanced diet is whether to give supplements. If vitamins and minerals are healthful, more of them must be better, right? Not necessarily. Too much of anything can cause problems.

For instance, puppies supplemented with calcium can develop deformed bones or have stunted growth. Too much calcium can also interfere with zinc absorption and cause a zinc deficiency. The result is a dog with skin problems, such as thinning or gray hair, spots where the skin is moist, or increased bacterial infections on the skin.

Too many vitamins can also cause problems. Excessive amounts of vitamin D and C are associated with an increased risk of a certain type of urinary stones. Too much vitamin A can suppress the immune system.

Chapter Four: Feeding Your Vizsla Dog

Most veterinary nutritionists agree that supplements aren't necessary if a dog eats a complete and balanced diet. Nonetheless, there are some circumstances in which supplements can be helpful. Dogs with skin problems often benefit from essential fatty acid (EFA) supplements, and older dogs, or dogs with health problems, may need certain supplements because they're less able to absorb nutrients. Of course a dog that's eating a homemade diet needs a multivitamin, which is usually recommended in recipes for homemade dog foods. Ask your veterinarian for advice before supplementing your Vizsla's diet.

Treat Talk

Like most of us, Vizslas love treats. Who doesn't enjoy something crunchy, savory, or sweet in addition to the healthy foods that make up our regular meals? Treats are super motivators during training sessions, and it's fun to give them on a dog's birthday, after a great performance at a flyball event, or just for being such a wonderful dog. As with all good things, however, moderation is the watchword.

What kind of treats do Vizslas like? You name it, they'll eat it. Hard biscuits and carrots satisfy the need for something crunchy, and both are good for the teeth. Frozen baby carrots can help soothe the sore gums of a teething puppy.

Many dogs also enjoy fruits, such as apples, bananas, and strawberries. Rather than giving your Vizsla sweet, fattening ice cream, choose the more healthful doggie ice cream that's available in the freezer section of grocery stores. Frozen vegetables are also refreshing on a hot summer day. Numerous dog bakeries offer cookies and cakes made just for dogs, with none of the sugar or chocolate that would be harmful to them.

Treats shouldn't make up more than 10 percent of your dog's daily food intake. Be aware of how much you're giving, and cut back a little on his food in the evening if you had an extra-long training session or a special event, such as a birthday with doggie cake.

For training treats, use foods that are small, smelly, and quickly eaten. Cut up some hot dogs or cubes of cheese. Cat treats are highly odorous and are just the right size for a training reward. Freeze-dried liver is another favorite, as are tiny bite-size biscuits.

For chewing pleasure, Vizslas love pig ears and rawhides. There's a risk of choking with these products, especially if your dog tends to gobble them down rather than gnaw on them for hours. Give them only while you're around to supervise.

Foods To Avoid

Are there any foods your Vizsla shouldn't eat? Absolutely! Chocolate, onions, grapes, raisins, and alcoholic beverages are among the items your dog should never ingest.

Chocolate may be the food of love, but it doesn't love dogs. A chemical in chocolate called theobromine is toxic to dogs and can cause vomiting, diarrhea, panting, restlessness, and muscle tremors. Too much chocolate can even kill a dog. Dark chocolate and unsweetened baking chocolate (which doesn't even taste good) contain more theobromine than candy, which is adulterated with sugars and other ingredients. Keep any form of chocolate well out of your Vizsla's reach.

Raw or cooked onions are off limits, too. A chemical in onions can destroy a dog's red blood cells, causing a serious or even fatal case of anemia.

Lots of dogs love grapes and they seem harmless enough, but grapes and raisins (dried grapes) have been reported to cause acute kidney failure in some dogs. It's not known why the sweet treats cause a problem, but it's best to avoid giving them to dogs. Signs of toxicity from eating grapes or raisins include vomiting within a few hours of eating them, loss of appetite, diarrhea, lethargy, and abdominal pain. These signs can last for days or even weeks. Successful treatment involves activated charcoal to help prevent absorption of toxins and hospitalization with intravenous fluids for at least two days. The veterinarian will monitor blood chemistry for three days to ensure that kidney failure doesn't develop.

You might be able to train your Vizsla to bring you a beer from the fridge, but don't share it with him. Getting a dog drunk isn't funny, it's dangerous. Alcoholic beverages can be harmful or even fatal to dogs.

Chapter Four: Feeding Your Vizsla Dog

Obesity

You might not ever have thought of obesity as a health problem, but it's linked to diabetes and orthopedic problems. Obesity is the most common health problem veterinarians see in dogs, and Vizslas are no exception. If they eat too much and don't get the exercise they need, they balloon up to resemble sausages on legs.

How Much Weight Is Too Much?

A Vizsla that's too fat weighs 15 percent or more above the normal weight for the breed (55 to 80 pounds, depending on the dog's gender). Because Vizslas enjoy their food so much, they're prone to obesity, so it's important to keep their weight normal by feeding measured amounts and providing plenty of exercise.

Chapter Five: Grooming Your Vizsla Dog

When a Vizsla is clean and his coat is shiny and well cared for, there isn't a more beautiful dog. But grooming your Vizsla isn't just for aesthetics. Grooming is a necessary part of caring for his health. Vizslas are easy to groom. Some may say that they're "wash and wear" dogs. They don't need clipping or expensive scissoring to have a beautiful coat. But there's still work to be done, and if you don't have time for grooming, you might want to consider other options.

Chapter Five: Grooming Your Vizsla Dog

Use a Groomer or Do It Yourself?

Considering that the Vizsla is easy to maintain, you may think that a groomer is a bit of a luxury. But a low-maintenance coat doesn't mean a no-maintenance coat. Vizslas are short coated. They require a minimum of a once-a-week brushing and a bath once a month or when they get dirty. If you are too busy to keep up with a grooming schedule, you might want to consider hiring a professional groomer. Groomers charge between $20 and $40, depending on what you want done.

To find a good groomer, ask your dog-owning friends for recommendations or contact your vet. Many vets have groomers on-site. If you still can't find a good groomer nearby, contact the National Dog Groomers Association of America at (412) 962-2711 and ask for members in your area.

Before you make an appointment with a groomer, you'll want to ask if she's comfortable working with Vizsla dogs. You'll also want to find out if the groomer uses tranquilizers. Some groomers do, and if your Vizsla has epilepsy or is particularly sensitive to medications, you may wish to look elsewhere. Some groomers use muzzles with aggressive or hard-to-handle dogs. If your Vizsla is old, you may wish to ask what provisions the groomer makes to see that an older dog is comfortable. Ask the groomer what services she'll perform and how much she charges. Some will only brush and bathe, but others will clean ears, clip toenails, and express anal sacs. It is important to know ahead of time.

Chapter Five: Grooming Your Vizsla Dog

Note: Your Vizsla should also be comfortable with strangers handling him. If he is aggressive toward strangers, you may want to reconsider your choice to take him to a groomer and groom him yourself until you can properly socialize him.

Visit the groomer. The grooming room should be clean and free of dirt (though if she has been busy, there might be hair and water on the floor). If the groomer uses crate dryers, she should check on the dogs frequently–leaving a dog in a crate dryer unattended can be fatal. Both the groomer and staff should be pleasant. They should handle the dogs with kindness and care, even if the dog becomes agitated. You should leave the groomer's place feeling as though this is a good place to bring your Vizsla.

Grooming Supplies

Regardless of whether you decide to use a groomer, you should still have grooming tools so you can groom your Vizsla yourself. These should include the following:

- Slicker brush
- Curry brush or Zoom Groom
- Short comb
- Flea comb
- Dog toenail clippers

Chapter Five: Grooming Your Vizsla Dog

- Styptic powder
- Dog shampoo and conditioner
- Otic solution
- Cotton balls
- Toothbrush for dogs
- Toothpaste for dogs

Two useful pieces of equipment are a hair dryer for dogs and a grooming table. Dog hair dryers use forced air, but they have no heat, so they won't burn your Vizsla's skin. Grooming tables are great for you because they help prevent injury by raising the dog to a manageable height.

Note: Don't use shampoo or conditioner for humans on dogs. They aren't correctly pH balanced for a dog's skin and can dry out your Vizsla's fur. Never use human toothpaste on dogs. The fluoride in human toothpaste is poisonous to dogs. Use only toothpaste specially formulated for dogs.

Brushing and Combing

You need to brush and comb your Vizsla at least once a week. If you're planning on bathing your Vizsla, you will first have to brush and comb him out to remove any dead hair

Chapter Five: Grooming Your Vizsla Dog

and dirt. Brushing and combing stimulates the hair and skin, making it healthy and distributing the skin's natural oils.

Start with the curry brush or Zoom Groom to clean the dust and dirt out of his coat. Use a short comb to comb through the coat once. Then, use a slicker brush to brush against the grain of your Vizsla's coat to loosen and remove any dead hair. Brush the hair back in place.

Removing Mats

Because of their short coats, Vizslas generally don't have trouble with mats. However, if your Vizsla hasn't been brushed in a while or has gotten something stuck in his fur, use a detangling solution and a comb or mat breaker to gently remove the mats. If the mats are severe, take your Vizsla to a groomer to have the mats removed. Sometimes mats have to be shaved out with electronic clippers.

Bathing

Bathe your Vizsla whenever he's dirty with a good shampoo that's pH balanced especially for dogs. Use tepid water. Water that is comfortable for you may be too hot for him, so lukewarm water is best. Most dogs hate bathing and will do anything they can to avoid it. Some pet-supply stores carry a suction cup that clips onto your Vizsla's collar and attaches to the tub's side. This works if he doesn't pull too

Chapter Five: Grooming Your Vizsla Dog

hard–otherwise, you may find him by the bathroom door begging to get out. If you have a sturdy handle in your bathroom, such as a handhold, you can tie his leash to it and clip his collar to it to hold him in place. If you do this, never leave your Vizsla unattended. He could accidentally strangle himself.

Note: Never bathe a Vizsla that hasn't been brushed out first or one that has mats. You need to comb out the dead hair and remove the mats before you bathe or you will have a worse problem.

After shampooing your Vizsla, follow up with a conditioner especially made for dogs. Be certain to rinse well. Shampoo and conditioner residue will collect dirt faster and can dry out and irritate your dog's skin.

Bathing Essentials

When you bathe your Vizsla, you'll want to bathe him in a draft-free area. During the wintertime, this means indoors, which may make washing interesting. Once you've thoroughly rinsed him, pat him down with towels and keep him warm until he dries. If you have a blow dryer made for dogs, you can use that on him. Never use a blow dryer made for humans. The hot air will burn your Vizsla.

Chapter Five: Grooming Your Vizsla Dog

The Dog Wash

There are now places where you can wash your dog for under $10. Some are in pet-supply stores but others are actual businesses that offer special areas for washing your dog. The places supply the soap, towels, and grooming implements as well as bathing tubs, grooming tables, and dog hair dryers. They are a low-cost alternative to paying a groomer and a low-mess alternative to bathing your Vizsla in your house.

Cleaning Ears

Dogs with ears that droop like the Vizsla's tend to be more prone to ear infections. You need to keep your Vizsla's ears clean and sweet-smelling by cleaning them when they're dirty or once a week.

Use a mild otic solution made for cleaning dogs' ears. Avoid solutions with medications and mite treatments as these can cause irritation. If you suspect an infection or mites, have your veterinarian look at your dog's ears. Squeeze a little otic solution into his ears and gently massage them. Use sterile gauze or sponges to wipe out the excess.

Your Vizsla may have an ear infection or mites if you observe the following:

- Ears are foul smelling.

- Vizsla paws or scratches his ears or shakes his head.
- Ears have an excessive red, black, or waxy buildup.
- Ears are crusty or red.

If your Vizsla has any of these symptoms, you should take him to the vet for the appropriate treatment.

Clipping Toenails

Most dog owners would rank clipping toenails right up there with root canals and tooth extractions. And with good reason. Most dogs hate getting their toenails clipped, and Vizslas are no exception. What makes matters worse is that Vizslas have toenails that blend with the coat color, which makes it impossible to see the quick. Consequently, inexperienced Vizsla owners accidentally cut the quick, which firmly cements a profound hatred of toenail clipping within their Vizsla's mind.

Question: What is the quick?

The quick is the blood supply for the nail. It is very sensitive and if cut will bleed a lot. If you accidentally cut into it, not only will you have a mess, but you'll also have a Vizsla that will never want you to touch his feet again.

There are two types of nail clippers: the guillotine variety and the scissors type. Both are good if they have sharp blades. The scissors type sometimes has a safety stop that helps gauge a safe amount of nail to snip off.

Handling His Feet

Your Vizsla may not wish you to handle his feet at first. In this case, get him used to your holding his feet by picking up one foot at a time and letting it go. Give him a treat when you're done. Practice this often, and slowly increase the amount of time you hold his foot. When you finally can hold his foot long enough to clip his nails, try it.

Trimming Your Vizsla's Toenails

Hold your Vizsla's foot and snip off a small portion of the nail. If you have a safety stop, use that as a guide. Clip each toenail, and don't forget to clip the dewclaws if he has them. Give him a treat afterward. You'll need to clip his toenails once a week.

If there's a trick to snipping black toenails, it is taking only a little bit at a time. Stop if the nail feels spongy or if your Vizsla acts uncomfortable. If you do hit the quick, pack the nail with styptic powder to stop the bleeding. Another device, which costs more than the clippers, is a nail grinder. Dogs that dislike the clippers sometimes tolerate the grinder far better.

Chapter Five: Grooming Your Vizsla Dog

The quick grows as the nail grows. If you don't cut your Vizsla's toenails, the quick will be correspondingly long. The way to reduce the toenail and shrink the quick is to keep the nails cut short just before the quick and let the quick recede. After a few days, the quick will have receded and you can trim some more nail.

If you're unsure about clipping your Vizsla's nails, ask your vet or groomer to show you how to do it.

Dental Hygiene

Dogs don't get cavities the way we do, but they can have dental problems, such as tartar buildup and gum disease. This is why it is very important for you to brush your Vizsla's teeth at least once a week, but preferably daily.

Brushing Your Vizsla's Teeth

Some dogs dislike having their mouths handled. If your Vizsla doesn't like you touching his mouth, you can start with just flipping his cheek flap up and then praising him and giving him a treat. Do this several times a day so that he becomes used to your touching his lips.

Note: If your Vizsla starts chewing on things he's not supposed to, consider making an appointment with the vet to

Chapter Five: Grooming Your Vizsla Dog

see if there's something wrong with his teeth. Dogs can't tell you it hurts, so they try to alleviate the pain by chewing.

Once he is used to your touching his mouth, get a washcloth and wet the corner. Hold the washcloth so that your index finger is on the corner. Flip up your Vizsla's lip and gently touch his gums with the corner of the washcloth. Give him a treat. Do this several times a day and gradually lengthen the time you touch his gums with the washcloth. If he tolerates that, try gently massaging his gums with the wet washcloth.

Once he lets you rub his gums, it is time for a toothbrush and toothpaste. Use a toothbrush specially made for pets (some slip over the fingers) and use special pet toothpaste. (Don't use human toothpaste because it is toxic to your Vizsla.) Most pet toothpastes are either malt or chicken flavored, so it'll be quite a treat. Brush his teeth in a circular motion, and don't forget to brush the gums as well. Your Vizsla doesn't have to rinse and spit.

The Need for Dentist

If you care for your Vizsla's teeth, it is less likely he'll have to visit the doggie dentist. Still, a variety of factors are involved in determining whether your Vizsla will have healthy teeth. These include:

- **Genetics–** Heredity plays a role in whether a dog has good teeth.
- **Diet–** A good diet can prevent some dental disease.

- **Disease–** Some diseases can actually weaken the enamel on the tooth.
- **Accidents or fights–** Teeth can be broken in an accident or a dogfight.
- **Dental care–** Brushing your Vizsla's teeth can keep the doggy dentist at bay.

Dental Problems

Even if your Vizsla has the best of teeth, you should still be on the lookout for dental problems. Signs of a possible dental problem include these:

- Lack of appetite
- Foul breath
- Swollen gums
- Change in chewing or eating habits
- Sudden grumpiness
- Red gums
- Chipped or broken tooth

Talk to your vet about dental hygiene and your Vizsla. He or she may be able to make recommendations for diet and brushing teeth.

Chapter Five: Grooming Your Vizsla Dog

Anal Sacs

Anal sacs, or the anal glands, are two glands that sit at the four and eight o'clock positions around a dog's anus. They are filled with stinky fluid and usually express themselves when a dog defecates. (Dogs can express their anal sacs when they're fearful or nervous.) However, they can become full or impacted.

Note: Dogs who scoot along the ground or bite their rumps may have full anal glands. If you decide to empty them, do it while you bathe your Vizsla. These glands can really squirt, and they're foul-smelling.

To express the anal glands, get some paper towels and fold them up into an absorbent square. Place them over your dog's anus and press at the four and eight o'clock positions. Keep your face away from there as it can really squirt. Throw away the paper towel and wash your Vizsla thoroughly. If your Vizsla still has problems with his anal sacs, he may have an impacted anal gland and your vet may have to clear it.

Removing Skunk Odor

If your Vizsla is skunked, you may have heard that using tomato juice will clean it right up. The tomato-juice myth has been around for a long time, even though it doesn't work. The truth is that the person who is bathing the dog in tomato juice gets used to the skunk smell (their olfactory senses have been overloaded) and eventually can't smell it.

Chapter Five: Grooming Your Vizsla Dog

Other home remedies, such as douche or dandruff shampoos, won't remove the smell either. Instead, purchase a good commercial skunk odor remover or use this do-it-yourself remedy:

- 1 quart hydrogen peroxide
- ¼ cup baking soda
- 1 tsp dog shampoo

Mix it together, and wash your Vizsla with it. Be careful and keep the solution out of his eyes. Rinse thoroughly. Throw out any leftover solution because it can explode if kept in a container. This really works, and he might end up smelling better than before he got skunked.

Note: Skunks are carriers of rabies. If your Vizsla catches and kills one, you may have more trouble than just the skunk odor. Handle the dead skunk with rubber gloves and bag it. Have the state health department check it for rabies, and talk to your vet about getting a rabies booster for your Vizsla.

Removing Sticky Substances

Depending on the substance, you can try corn oil to loosen a sticky substance and wash it clean from your Vizsla. Otherwise, if it is tar or a petroleum-based substance, you will have to use a degreaser such as Dawn dishwashing liquid, GOOP, or Orange Power. If you're worried about the chemicals, be aware that many dishwashing detergents with

Chapter Five: Grooming Your Vizsla Dog

degreasers are actually excellent at removing petroleum products. They're often used on seabirds caught in oil slicks. Dawn is the mildest and is very effective. The two others mentioned are excellent at removing grease, but they are irritants. Be sure to bathe your Vizsla and wash all traces of the substance from his coat and skin.

Chapter Five: Grooming Your Vizsla Dog

Chapter Six: Training and Behavior Modification

Obedience Training

The very first thing you need to train your Vizsla is obedience; you cannot teach anything else successfully if the dog cannot obey you. The professionals say that although obedience training doesn't solve all dog problems, it is the very foundation of solving any dog problem.

In essence, obedience training involves teaching the dog such commands like sit, stop barking, off the couch, come, etc. In simpler terms, you train your dog to be obedient, to follow rules, and to behave in a particular manner. The training covers some skills such as family manners, new tricks, skills, demonstrations, or show ring exercises. You train the dog to obey a particular set of commands to increase productivity and relationship with people. The following are common obedience skills:

How to Teach a Dog to Sit

The sit command is the most fundamental training that should probably begin with before getting to other exercises. To train your dog on how to sit, follow these steps:

1. Get a treat and reveal it to your dog

2. Once the dog notices it and is interested, he or she should follow the treat with the head to get it.

3. Hold the treat above his or her head as he or she observes, and then put it on the nose. This ensures that the dog has to move the head backward, as the easiest way for the dog to reach the treat is by being on the floor.

4. After he or she puts his or her bottom on the floor, press your clicker and now present the treat with praises and lots of attention.

5. After a few attempts, the dog should learn how easy it is to get clicks and treats, which means that the sit response would probably be faster.

6. After a few successful attempts to make the dog sit using the gift, you can now introduce the word "sit"

Chapter Six: Training and Behavior Modification

when telling the dog to sit. This will make sure that the dog starts associating the sit command with sitting.

With time, your dog should be in a position to sit just from the command rather than having to give treats to make him or her sit.

How to Teach the Dog to Come

Training the dog, the "come" command is very critical if you really want to manage any annoying behaviors since you can use the command to keep the dog out of trouble. For instance, if he or she escapes the fenced yard or even bolts out an open door, you will definitely find the come command very helpful. To teach the dog to come, follow the following steps:

1. Start by clipping a light line to the dog's collar then let him or her drag it around the training ground (it could be a house or a backyard).

2. Then after he or she is accustomed to that line, you can then pick up one end then hold it as you follow the dog around the training ground. After he or she gets used to this, they will start noticing that the two of you are attached. Now use the marker word "yes" coupled with a few treats then walk backward as you encourage the dog to follow you.

3. As he or she follows you, ensure to say yes and give him a treat.

Chapter Six: Training and Behavior Modification

4. As the dog follows, start pairing this with the word "come" and when he or she responds correctly, you can then reward him and praise him; ensure to make this some sort of a game that the dog wants to play all the time.

Note: Don't have the habit of yelling come! Come! Come! Many times just to get the dog's attention-use one word for one command to ensure you don't end up confusing the dog. So if the dog doesn't get the first time, go over to him or her then gently guide him or her wherever you want him or her to go. Don't expect too much too soon.

Also, ensure you don't call the dog to come for discipline. Otherwise, you will make him or her associate the command with a negative consequence. So if the dog is behaving badly, don't call him or her for punishment; instead, go over to him or her.

"Lie Down" Command

The lie-down command is very handy if you want to instill manners in your dog since it helps you to control the dog's impulses and ultimately control the dog. For instance, the dog won't be able to do such things like jumping up, begging at the table, knocking over the kids, chasing the cat, running off, or dashing out of the door or even counter surfing if he or she is lying down. This only means that a dog in a down position is definitely a good dog! Same as the "sit" command, teaching the dog how to lie down is important on some occasions. The "down" command should only be used to make the dog lie

Chapter Six: Training and Behavior Modification

down. Thus, you shouldn't confuse with other commands. If you want the dog to come off the sofa, use a different command to say "Off." Follow these easy and efficient steps to teach your dog the "lie down" command:

1. Find a training spot that is free of any distractions then ask the puppy/dog to sit; yes, it starts with the sit command.

2. Have a treat in your hand and ensure it sticks out to ensure the dog notices it

3. Let the dog almost lick it (not eat) then say "down" as you slowly bring your hand down to the ground right between the dog's front paws. If the dog gets to the down position instantly, congratulate him or her and give him a treat. You can also press the clicker if you have it. Having a clicker is great in training since it produces the exact same sound repeatedly. This means that the dog can never be confused when he or she hears the clicker. It is very likely that in your celebratory mood, you end up saying or doing things that only serve to confuse the dog!

4. Ensure to keep your hand on the floor while covering the food then try to give him a few moments to figure it out. This should make the dog lower their body in an attempt to get the treat.

Repeat the exercise several times then as the dog continues to understand the command, ensure to start pairing the actions with "down". You can then start introducing duration between getting down and the time you give the

Chapter Six: Training and Behavior Modification

reward (well, don't make it too long though), distance from the treat to the dog and distractions to ensure the dog can still make out the command in the midst of all these situations.

Note: If the dog doesn't stand automatically after eating the treat, you can move a step further to encourage him or her to move out of the down position then ensure to repeat this for about 20 times.

Tip: If the dog doesn't follow your treat, it is probable that he or she doesn't like it so try to look for something different; you can get a piece of chicken, hot dog, etc.

Tip: If the dog's back end pops up whenever you try to get him to the down position, ensure to snatch the treat then get him or her to try again.

You can introduce a hand signal to show the dog to go to the down position. To do this, ensure to start with the sit position then say down as you use a hand motion to show the dog to sit you don't need a treat on your hand to do this. If the dog gets it right, only clap your hands or move back a few steps to encourage the dog to stand. Repeat this for about 20 times or until the dog gets it right all the time.

Train the "No" Command

This command is useful in making the dog realize when he or she makes mistakes. The easiest way to teach dogs this command is making them respond by stopping all activities when you say "no." Follow these steps to teach this command.

Chapter Six: Training and Behavior Modification

1. Place a treat on the floor, and let the dog attempt to eat it. Then rattle 5 metal disks or dog training disks in your hand. As you rattle the disks, withdraw the treat without saying anything, only letting the sound do its work. The sound made by the disk is different from other sounds the dog previously encountered. The dog should learn that, unlike the click that means a treat, the sound from the disk means no treat.

2. Repeat this practice until the dog isn't startled by the sound but instead links it with not getting a reward. With time, the dog won't even attempt to take treats after the sounds from the disk. He or she will give up and get disappointed.

3. Then let the dog do other commands that warrant a treat such as "Sit" or "Down" to calm and restore the happy feeling in them. With time, the dog should link the actions or situations where he or she encounters the disk with failure and thus stop them.

Train Your Dog To "Stay."

This exercise could prove the hardest, as most dogs don't prefer being still though you can manage it through short and regular activities. The training is sufficient in cases such as your dog diving out of your car before you put her leash on.

1. Begin with the "Down" command and then say "Stay" in a steady voice as you place your hand out in front of you with the palm facing forward.

2. After a few seconds, press your clicker and then reward your dog for staying still, and repeat the exercise a number of times.

3. Later, say the "Down" command; step back and then say "Stay". Wait for a few seconds, click and step forward to reward him or her. Also, praise your dog for being brilliant.

Continue to increase your length and distance of "stay" but in a gradual process. In case your dog doesn't comply with the command, don't shout but rather don't click or reward him or her. Within a few days, your dog should get used to staying still.

Train Your Dog To "Get Off."

1. When you find your dog on the couch, say "Off", and then encourage him or her to come to greet you.

2. Once the dog approaches, reward him or her with praises as you press the clicker. Use the obedience commands to instruct him or her to "sit" or go "down", and reward him or her if necessary.

If your dog doesn't get off from the couch, use your hands to remove him or her and then tell him "Off." Ensure you are consistent with these cues, and all family members are accustomed to them. If the dog growls or attempts to "refuse" being removed from the couch, you might require assistance from a qualified behaviorist.

Chapter Six: Training and Behavior Modification

Do not try to force training on a troublesome or stubborn dog as you might make things worse.

The "Leave It" Command

This command is similar to "No!" command and is applicable if your dog likes sniffing or touching things in your house. You might need to have some dog training disks to make the lessons useful.

1. Place an item on the table where a dog can reach, and then say "Leave it." Then count 1-3 and give him a treat, but a different gift than the one you had placed on the table.

2. In case he or she reaches for the treat, rattle or sound your training discs.

As you continue with training sessions, increase the duration the dog has to wait before being praised or given a treat.

Potty Training

The secret of how to potty train puppies is perseverance, patience, active reinforcement, and proper arrangement. Most puppies will learn a training schedule within 4 to 6 months. If they are under 24 weeks of age, they need to go to the toilet at least 3 to 5 times a day.

Chapter Six: Training and Behavior Modification

Fast and reliable potty training methods may be the most needed resource for every new puppy owner. If you are to start this business, this training will make your life easier. Although the core of potty training is a simple process, it may be full of misunderstandings and frustrations. Therefore, you need to be a responsible and patient master and slowly teach it to learn. In the end, you will find that your dog will rely on you more and more and will be very obedient. You can master potty training skills by following these steps and tips. I hope it will help you. There is only one acceptable method of potty training for dogs of any age: active reinforcement.

Remember, dogs don't treat their poop like we do. For them, peeing and pooping can be very fun! Punishing your dog for entering the house will not help him understand what he should do but may make him afraid of getting close to you inside or outside. Successful potty training requires patience, kindness, and remember that your dog is learning the rules, just like a toddler.

Before starting potty training, prepare for multiple trips outdoors throughout the day. The best way to teach puppies to go out is to persevere. Once a routine is done, all dogs can quickly understand what to expect.

Steps:

This simple guide will teach you how to train a puppy to potty in a specific area patiently.

1. Get up as early as possible and take the puppy outdoors.

Chapter Six: Training and Behavior Modification

2. Place your puppy in the designated potty spot, and don't let the puppy go away.
3. Let the puppy smell the ground and explore until they find a suitable location (within the designated area).
4. After a successful potty time, reward your puppy with snacks or petting and praising.
5. Go back indoors and get breakfast for your puppy.
6. Twenty minutes after eating/drinking/playing, take the puppy outside again.
7. Place your puppy in the same position he marked earlier. Let him explore again.
8. To help him understand that it's time to go to the potty, slowly let him walk around the area and encourage him to follow you. As soon as the puppy begins to defecate, use a command, such as "go potty," in a natural tone.
9. Repeat the command and point to the area he is going to. This may require some attempts.
10. Once the puppy has learned this, give him many compliments; you can even give him a small reward.
11. After 2 hours, repeat steps 7 to 10.
12. Dog training skills: stay consistent, never miss a rest, always support your puppy, you will get the results you want soon!

How long does it take to train a puppy to sit down?

Some puppies receive potty training within six months, but it may take longer. Like most young people, it is important for puppies to learn at their own pace and to have patience, kindness, and support in toilet training.

Chapter Six: Training and Behavior Modification

The bladder control of a puppy depends on its size, breed, and age. Smaller species require increased potty trips because their bodies process food and liquids much faster than larger breeds.

From the first day of the puppies potty training program, please make sure you are consistent so that he knows that he will go out after a nap, recreation time, food, or any activity. Most puppies need to relieve their needs every few hours, regardless of their breed.

Use a baby gate to limit the puppy's range of activities if you don't have a dog pen or designated area. Pay attention to potty diving indicators, such as sniffing or hovering. Puppies need to evacuate five times or more a day. Dogs under six months of age should rotate their potty 2 hours a day. Once the puppy has used the designated potty location, give him many compliments to reward him for his excellent behavior. Do not punish puppies for indoor errors, and do not yell or fight with them. If the puppy has an accident, firmly say "no" and gently pick him up or show him the potty location. To ensure that the puppies do not return to the same position inside, eliminate odors and clean them thoroughly.

Crate Training

When people hear crate training, the typical first thought is that you are imprisoning your dog, which is a wrong perception of the training. By crate training your dog, you are teaching it to be obedient, patient, and responsible. I

Chapter Six: Training and Behavior Modification

would rather have a dog well trained than a messy dog that doesn't care about anything. This type of training, like any other, takes time, it can take up to six months, but patience and persistence are rewarded.

You don't want the dog to see the crate as a punishment or a negative area; if you put the dog for the first time in the crate for hours, they will see it as a jail. So instead, start with 7 minutes one day, and then add more minutes every day; that way, the dog will get used to spending time in the crate in a progressive manner.

The crate should be as comfortable as possible; make sure you learn what your dog prefers to lay on, such as a dog bed, towels, blankets, or other items. Once you know what they like, put their favorite things inside the crate to make it as comfortable as possible and let them know that it is a safe place to relax.

Give them treats when they go in the crate. You have to do this, especially at the beginning of the training; this way, the dog can associate being in the crate positively. One thing that works well, especially after a bit of training, is freezing a treat. The dog will have to work to get to the treat while being in the crate, reinforcing that spending time in the crate is a good thing.

Be aware of how much time in the crate your dog is going to spend. Dogs have physiological needs like bathroom, eating, and playing; you don't want to restrain a dog for too long from any of these needs.

Chapter Six: Training and Behavior Modification

When leaving the dog in the crate for long periods, a good thing to do is to record them. If you happen to have a camera, you can set up the device so you can see your dog's behavior while you are not there. This will help you know and understand your dogs' experience in the crate to make adjustments.

Unwanted Behavior

We've covered the basics of Vizsla dog training, and gone into particular approaches. If all has gone well, you and your dog have sailed right through the training and your dog is responding to a number of commands, reliably and well.

And it may be that the training is running into some challenges. Here are some guidelines for what to do when you encounter dog training issues or unwanted behaviors.

Your Dog's Instinctive Response to Authority

A well-trained dog is a superior companion whose training keeps him, and others, safe from harm. The training can truly be a factor of life or death, for both your dog and for others that his behavior might impact. It's no accident that many professional trainers are most often called in to address a dog who is aggressive, and who can't interact properly with the family, other humans, or other animals.

Chapter Six: Training and Behavior Modification

Ironically, understanding your dog's genetic background as a wild creature will help you understand how to better domesticate him into the obedient companion animal that will be rewarding to both of you.

The beginning of dogs' domestication was likely when orphaned wolf cubs were adopted by early humans. The relationship wasn't too far from what it is today – the dogs were appealing, loving, loyal. They needed food and shelter, and humans provided that in return for things the dogs could provide that the humans valued, such as support in hunting, help driving off predators, and serving as early warning signals when danger was approaching. Today, working and herding dogs, police dogs and dog performers still perform valuable work for their human owners.

You'll have a better instinct about training your dog and respond to challenges better when you remember your dog's background as a member of a pack. Wild dogs and wolves form packs with a specific hierarchy. Every animal in the pack knows his place in that hierarchy and knows what to expect in terms of the associated responsibilities and expected behaviors.

The entire pack defers to the leadership of the alpha dog. The alpha makes the call on choices around hunting, food, and whether to avoid other animals or engage in conflict with them. To our human minds, it might seem the alpha dog was an enemy to be overcome; but in truth, pack members feel confident and relaxed when they have a strong alpha leader they can trust. Your dog will be more stable and happier if you are a strong alpha leader for him. He will see you as a superior, and will follow your commands – the more he perceives you as alpha, the more likely he is to follow commands quickly and without question.

Dog Training for Desired Behaviors

It just makes sense that it's easier to train your dog in the behaviors you want than it is to correct bad behavior. So do you and your dog a favor – invest in quality training time with him, on a regular basis.

That's especially true when you have a young dog. It's not all work – as we've said, even when you have unstructured play time with your puppy, he's learning. But it's also important to engage in formal training to teach your puppy what you expect from him, and which behaviors are acceptable to you, and which are not.

If you take the time to teach these lessons when your puppy is young, it's more likely he'll learn them quickly, and retain the lessons. Remember – every experience your puppy has teaches him something. Make sure his experiences are teaching him well and reinforcing the things you want him to know, and the behaviors you want to see.

The strong bond that dogs form with humans is one of your biggest assets in training your dog. That bond is based on relationships humans have had with dogs for thousands of years; the dog's ability to form that relationship made his

Chapter Six: Training and Behavior Modification

survival more likely, so the qualities of respect, affection and obedience were preserved just by virtue of natural selection.

Also useful in your approaches to training your dog are the dynamics of pack hierarchy, and your position as the leader of your dog's pack. Make it a point to use that hierarchy when you train your dog. In setting yourself up as the leader of your dog's pack, you gain his trust and his respect. Conversely, if your dog does not recognize you as his superior, and a leader worthy of his respect, your training will be much more difficult, if not impossible.

How do you gain and keep that respect? It can't be forced. Rather, it is earned by your interactions with your dog. Using the reward or positive reinforcement approach to training teaches the dog to respect you and trust you, far more than he would if you based your interactions on fear and intimidation. As noted previously – fear causes your dog to exhibit aggressive behavior, such as biting.

Because of that, punishing your dog only frightens and confuses him; one bad episode can set your training back weeks, even months. It's an interactive process to train your dog well, giving him the option to choose to do what you ask of him, and rewarding him with praise, treats or other positive elements when he makes the right decision. If, for example, your dog chases people, arrange to have a friend jog past while you have your dog on leash. Your dog has a choice: he can refrain from chasing the jogger, and if he does, you should reward him. If he chases him, sit him back down and start the exercise again, until he understands.

Chapter Six: Training and Behavior Modification

It isn't about punishing him for the wrong decision. It is about rewarding him for choosing to respond in accordance with what you want from him. Always keep in mind that rewarding your dog, rather than punishing him, will be far more likely to result in a well-trained – and happy – dog, and a satisfied owner.

Your Dog's Motivation for Behaving Badly

There are a number of reasons why people train their dogs. There are practical reasons, such as ensuring the safety of the dog and those around him. But there are softer reasons as well – the joy that a well-trained dog and its owner find in each other, the companionship, loyalty, and love.

Bad behavior doesn't usually indicate your dog is a hopeless miscreant. If you take the time to understand the reason for his behaviors and address them accordingly, you can still have the companion animal you want him to be – it just may take a bit more time and effort. For example, it's easy to be frustrated when your dog chews your new furniture; it's easier to understand his behavior if you realize it's in response to his separation anxiety. In training to offset bad behaviors, it's important to address the root cause – the anxiety – rather than the behavior itself – the chewing.

In fact, very often your dog's behavior may look aggressive or thoughtless, but it's in response to his inability to cope with anxiety. You might think you need to reduce the stress he feels, and certainly that's helpful; but more often, the best approach is to engage in a training program that teaches him to better tolerate and deal with the stress.

By now, you've probably observed that what motivates a human, and human behavior, can be very different from the things that motivate a dog, and dog behavior. And from what you've read so far, you may have come to the realization that a good handler doesn't just train his dog in good behavior – he's also training himself to be the kind of trainer that leads to having an obedient dog. When trying to understand your dog's behavior, don't confuse his motivations with those of a human. Sure, he may seem almost human at times, particularly if he's especially intelligent. But even if he understands things in the way a human would, his motivations are different, as are his responses to situations and challenges.

So, modulate your thinking and your behaviors to remember that your dog is a dog – not a human. Just as you remember the things humans and dogs share – the need for relationships and close bonds with those in the pack family.

Refusing to Come when Called

If your relationship with your dog isn't all you'd like, take a moment to ask if your problems hearken back to your dog's training on coming when you call. Not only does "come when called" impact a number of other behaviors; failing to come when he's called to you can result in dangerous situations you're unprepared for, such as having a collar

Chapter Six: Training and Behavior Modification

break near heavy traffic, or your dog bolting and getting free to chase a person or a cat. Consider for a moment the possible legal repercussions of your dog's failure to come when called, or the possibility that his uncontrolled impulsiveness could actually prove fatal to him.

Your dog learns from what he's allowed to do. When you allow him to run off leash and indulge himself in whatever behavior he likes, you're damaging any training you've done that teaches him to look to you – not himself – for what he does and the choices he makes. Running loose in a park, or on the beach, or with other dogs is fun; probably more fun than things you'd rather he was doing. Some dogs can handle free time, are aware when the handler is changing the parameters to be about obedience, and can adjust. If your dog cannot adjust, you need to limit how much free, impulsive time he has to practice behaviors and choices that don't involve your commands.

You can understand, if you put yourself in your dog's place. Picture him doing the things he loves, like running wild on the beach – imagine you're the dog, for a second. The waves are rolling in, you're chasing them, there are other dogs running free, and you're chasing them too, and roughhousing with them. And – oh, no. Here comes your handler, wanting you to obey, for Pete's sake. Taking the fun out of everything. Killjoy! Seen from that perspective, you can understand why a dog might grow resistant to leash, collar, and training.

What to do? One likely approach your dog might take is just to ignore you when you call and refusing to come. And

Chapter Six: Training and Behavior Modification

now you're in a rough spot because your dog has learned there's a reward for him – fun, and freedom – in ignoring you.

If your dog has not yet realized the potential ignoring you has, do yourself a favor and don't let him learn it. It's a lot easier to prevent this learned behavior than it is to work with him to un-learn it.

If he has already learned it – as is likely, if you're reading this section of the book – your approach should be to supervise his play and make the time you spend with your dog fun, so he associates your call with something positive, rather than with something that limits his good time.

You won't reprogram your dog by following "Come" with something unpleasant, so try not to do that. Don't call him and then give him a bath, clip his nails or do something else he really doesn't like, or you'll be teaching him if he comes when called, he's going to regret it.

Instead, call him and then give him a toy, a treat, or some playtime with you. Use some other command to get his attention when there's something unpleasant in store for him.

Remember – your dog is constantly learning. He's learning when you're training him in obedience – but he's also learning when you call him, and he comes and is sorry, and learning when he's having fun and you call him and he ignores you – the fun continues. So approach your relationship with him as though every interaction is laying the groundwork you want to secure his attention and his obedience.

Chapter Six: Training and Behavior Modification

And remember the key to training him – positive reinforcement. Just make it a habit to reward your dog each and every time he shows the behavior and obedience you want. Certainly, if you're having training issues, you may need to rely on treats that are irresistible – generally, yummy bits of tasty food. But dogs are sensitive to energy, so the reward can be a simple scratch behind the ears or a "Yeah, good boy!" When teaching the dog to come on command, it is vital that the dog be consistently rewarded every single time he does as the owner wants. A reward can be as simple as a pat on the head, a "good boy" or a scratch behind the ears. Whatever the reward, be consistent in giving something positive every time you call your dog and he comes.

Eliminating Biting Behaviors

Puppies are impulsive and enthusiastic. Those qualities are what make them such a joy – and can also make them challenging. Puppies are prone to chewing and biting. Here are some approaches to curbing biting behaviors.

Preventing Biting and Mouthing

Puppies and young dogs are often prone to biting and mouthing. It's natural for a puppy to bite and mouth its siblings when playing, and when you play with your puppy, it's natural for him to play that way with you, too. But puppies have thick skin; humans do not, and those sharp little

Chapter Six: Training and Behavior Modification

puppy teeth can be a problem. So it's important to let your puppy know when his approaches to playing with you are appropriate, and when they are not.

A puppy's mother and its siblings would ordinarily teach him what biting behavior is appropriate, and what is not. But since puppies are now taken away from their mothers at a younger age, your puppy may have missed out on that mother/puppy training.

So, it's up to you to train your puppy by inhibiting his reflex to bite. Don't let biting continue just because it's not a big problem now; your little 5-pound puppy is going to grow, and what is a small problem now could very well become a big problem later. To ensure your adult dog won't have biting and mouthing problems, teach your puppy to control his urge to bite before he reaches the age of four months.

You can tap back into the natural way of teaching the puppy, by letting him interact and socialize with older dogs or other active puppies. If you've watched puppies with other puppies and dogs, you'll notice they bite each other almost constantly when playing. The puppies are testing limits; they bite harder until another puppy or dog reacts in a negative way, growling or snapping or biting back. That's how a puppy learns what's appropriate and acceptable, and what isn't. Through this kind of play, your puppy will learn some of the lessons that help him control his biting reflex. Even so – his little teeth don't hurt the thicker skin of other dogs and puppies the same way it will hurt a human, so you may need to give him additional lessons in what's appropriate with you.

Chapter Six: Training and Behavior Modification

Using Trust to Prevent Biting

The more your puppy trusts and respects you, the less problem you're likely to have with biting. At the least, a trusting and respectful relationship will let you address biting problems more easily and effectively. Indeed, all dog training is impacted by the level of trust and respect your dog has for you.

Your dog's level of trust in you is severely damaged if and when you hit or slap it. The reason this book emphasizes training that is positive and rewarding is that it fosters a trusting relationship and bond between dog and owner – and that relationship, in turn, makes training easier and more effective. Nothing erodes your relationship with your dog like physical punishment. In terms of biting behaviors, reprimanding your dog for biting may be your first instinct, but it will only scare and confuse your dog, and it won't do anything to alter his behavior. Stay positive with your training – always.

Eliminating Bad Habits

If you have a dog or puppy, it's like any relationship – there will be times that things don't go quite as you'd like them to. Any owner of a dog or puppy will sometimes find themselves needing to work with the dog to alter behavior of some sort. Most dogs love their owner and see him or her as

Chapter Six: Training and Behavior Modification

their pack leader; a dog's nature is to want to please their pack leader, and dogs are sufficiently smart enough to do so if you clearly communicate what is acceptable and unacceptable. In other words, your dog will very likely do what you want him to do, providing he knows and understands what you expect.

The approach to shifting unwanted behavior depends on the behavior itself, and, to some extent, the nature and character of your dog. Each dog is different; there are similarities among dogs of a certain breed, of course, but even so, each dog is an individual, and you may need to try a couple of approaches before you find the best approach to eliminating unwanted behavior.

Whining, Howling and Excessive Barking

Dogs are usually vocal, and in fact, were almost certainly valued for their ability to bark and warn humans of danger. Both dogs and puppies are natural barkers and may howl and whine, and that's normal. But at some point, it can become a problem. It's particularly challenging if you live in an apartment or home very close to your neighbor. Your neighbors have a right to expect that your dog won't always be disturbing their peace with the sounds he makes.

What to do? Here are some tips to control excessive barking and other vocalizations:

- Your dog may be whining to tell you it truly needs something; for example, if your dog or puppy is crated

Chapter Six: Training and Behavior Modification

and begins to howl or whine, take it to its toilet area. The dog may be letting you know it needs to do its business.

- In addition to needing to relieve itself, the dog may be whining for other reasons, so check to be sure he has water and isn't ill. Check to see his toy isn't out of reach under a chair, and that the temperature isn't too hot or cold.
- In addition to physical needs, be sure your dog is getting all the affection and attention he needs to feel confident and loved. Also, make sure he has toys to keep himself occupied.
- Training emphasizes building a bond by spending time together, but there are times (perhaps often) that your dog will need to be left in the home alone. It's part of pack behavior for your dog to want you to be with him, and if you are gone, he may suffer from separation anxiety, which can lead to such behaviors as destroying furniture and incessant barking. Work to accustom your puppy to being left alone.
- Be careful that in being responsive to your dog's needs, you don't inadvertently reward him for unwanted behavior. For example, if he whines, don't go to him and give him attention – that only reinforces his tendency to whine. Instead, once you've made sure his physical needs are met and that he is comfortable and has what he needs by way of toys, it is appropriate to scold him for whining, letting him know that whining is unwanted behavior.

Chapter Six: Training and Behavior Modification

Problem Chewing

Just as you can expect your puppy to vocalize, you can also expect him to chew. Puppies use their mouth, tongue, and teeth to explore their world. Just because chewing is normal, however, that doesn't mean it's acceptable behavior; "normal" is not a reason to be OK with your puppy chewing your new leather boots. Address unwanted chewing early, so your chewing puppy doesn't become a big, chewing dog.

Chewing itself is OK, and it's fine to encourage your dog to chew appropriate items, such as his toys. Giving your dog a variety of chew toys helps keep him entertained, makes him feel safe in that he can satisfy a need in a way that is acceptable, and help him keep his teeth and gums clean and exercised.

To reinforce the "OK to chew/not OK to chew" guideline for your puppy, encourage him to play with his chew toys. Praise him for playing with them and chewing with them. If you find him chewing something inappropriate, gently take it away, and hand him a toy; then praise him when he pays attention to and chews the toy.

Another way you can encourage him to play with his toys and chew them, and let him know you approve, is to take advantage of his enthusiasm when he greets you. As you come in the door and the puppy runs to you, put your things down, hand him one of his toys, and praise him for taking it. You can also encourage him to go get one of his toys every time he greets you.

Chapter Six: Training and Behavior Modification

Your puppy's toys should be easily accessible; he will probably be drawn to chew on anything and everything that's accessible all his life, so keep things picked up and out of his reach. In particular, try to keep things that carry your scent – shoes, hairbrushes, used tissues – out of his reach.

If you witness your puppy picking up something he shouldn't have, such as a sock, distract him with another toy as you take the sock away. When he takes the toy, be sure to praise him for playing with it and chewing on it.

If the chewing continues, you can try taking an item you are certain the dog knows you do not want him to chew; putting something bad-tasting but non-toxic on it, such as hot pepper sauce; and leaving it for him to find. The unpleasant reaction he has should help train him to only chew on items you've told him are appropriate.

Jumping On People

You've probably been jumped on by a friend's dog, and wish you hadn't been. It's a common behavior, and one owners often express a wish to change. Changing this behavior is certainly possible, but it's harder to change it if you encouraged it when your puppy was young, and only now find it less appealing. If you reward your 10-pound puppy's jumping on you with kisses or treats, you probably realize by now that your actions are reinforcing the dog's bad behavior and it won't be so appealing when he grows to 100 pounds. If it isn't already too late, start training your young

Chapter Six: Training and Behavior Modification

dog that jumping on people is not acceptable behavior, as retraining is time-consuming, confusing for your dog, and can be difficult.

Your dog's tendency to jump on people is more than an inconvenient annoyance; it's dangerous. Even a smaller dog can knock a human off balance, especially a child or older adult. Not only does your poorly trained dog embarrass you and pose a threat to others – but it also puts you at risk of being targeted in a lawsuit.

To train your puppy not to jump, whenever the dog jumps on you or someone else, you should gently put his feet back down on the floor. Once all four of his feet are on the floor – and remain there – load on the praise! For the sake of your puppy's training, ask everyone in the family to follow this procedure if the puppy jumps on them. You can even ask guests to get with the program! Because if you don't accept this behavior, but the puppy's impression is that others do, he'll be confused about what appropriate behavior is regarding jumping on people. Consistency is definitely a plus when it comes to dog training – consistency not just from you, but from others in the family.

Straining and Pulling at the Leash

Your puppy is probably enthusiastic and eager – one of the things we love about them is their unflagging zest for life. But his enthusiasm can sometimes result in him being overly eager and pulling on the leash.

Chapter Six: Training and Behavior Modification

Your first goal is not to initiate or encourage pulling on the leash by playing tug-of-war with your puppy with the leash, or anything that resembles a leash, like a length of rope. Instead, choose a toy in the shape of a ring if you want to play tug-of-war with him.

If your puppy pulls and you are having trouble training him not to, consider using a body harness. When choosing a harness, try it on your dog before purchasing; some dogs have a particular body type that may make finding a harness that fits a challenge; for example, corgis can be particularly long from ears to shoulders, making it hard to fit them in a harness.

Practice good habits when walking your dog, encouraging him to keep his head level with your knee and to walk by your side. A well-fitted training collar or choke chain can help your dog understand just where you want his head to be.

Don't continuously pull back on the leash when your puppy pulls ahead. Instead, quickly change directions to make your puppy suddenly fall behind you. Anticipate the puppy and change directions before he reaches the end of the leash, or you could put too much pressure on his neck when your direction changes. Keep the leash loose except for that moment when your direction changes – you should feel a slight tug on the leash, and then loosen it immediately.

Never pull or yank the puppy's neck to correct him. You should apply steady pressure, gently, rather than a hard yank. Aim to use the least amount of pressure possible to get

Chapter Six: Training and Behavior Modification

your puppy headed in the right direction, in the correct position.

Just as you don't want to play tug-of-war with the leash, don't let your puppy pull on the leash and pull you around. Consistency in how you use the leash – what it is and is not for – is essential to teaching the dog how to use it properly. If you have a dog that is going to be very large, take particular advantage of his smaller puppy-years to train him to the leash, because it will be a lot easier now than when he weighs 150 pounds.

Escaping and Roaming

Can you imagine letting your dog out the front door to roam up and down the street, and from yard to yard? Just the thought of what could happen probably takes your breath away – the dangers from cars, encounters with other animals, adventures with open garbage cans and other possible incidents probably make your imagination run wild.

It is illegal in most towns for dogs to roam free, and a roaming dog is likely to be picked up by animal control - which is almost certain to be unpleasant, expensive and dangerous for your dog.

But if the thought of your dog roaming free scares the dickens out of you, it's a pretty sure bet your dog sees it differently. Outside your fence or out your front door are an array of scents and sounds that most dogs are just dying to

Chapter Six: Training and Behavior Modification

investigate further, and if your dog can escape your yard or your house – and you haven't trained him not to – he almost certainly will.

Preventing his escape is much easier – and much safer – than it is to try to recapture a dog that's gotten loose. So here are some precautions and preventative measures you can take, ahead of time, to keep your dog on your premises.

First, do what you can to keep your dog engaged where he is – if he's bored, he's much more likely to investigate ways to get out and entertain himself. So surround him with all the things he might need – a warm, soft bed, a filled water bowl and plenty of toys, and your dog will likely spend some time playing, take a nice long drink of water, and flop over in his bed to rest and dream – safe and sound.

It's also a really good approach to exercise your dog regularly, to use up all that energy he might otherwise use to escape. Especially for an energetic dog or a very intelligent one that gets bored easily, schedule lots of high-energy play sessions several times a day, and at least one good, long walk. It's especially good to wear the dog out right before you leave the house. Again – he's likely, then, to just seek out his bed and sleep till you return.

Next, address your house and fence and make sure you've done all you can to make it escape-proof. If your dog digs, you may need to extend the fence a few inches into the ground. If he jumps, your fence will need to be higher. If a deeper fence or a higher one are not enough to keep him in, you may need to never let him outside without supervision,

Chapter Six: Training and Behavior Modification

and confine him to the inside of the house, if you aren't going to be at home. Do whatever you need to do to ensure he doesn't get out to roam because a roaming dog is in danger and the result could truly be heartbreaking.

Socializing

Most Vizslas, when properly and continually socialized, will be tolerant of other dogs and respectful to people, however, this does may come naturally, therefore, it will be very important to expose them to different people, animals, places and unfamiliar sights and sounds when they are puppies.

Much of how any dog behaves will depend entirely upon you, how extensively they were socialized as a puppy and how much they are continually being socialized throughout their life because without proper socialization, even the most naturally friendly dog can become neurotic, unsociable and learn to act out aggressively toward unknown dogs or people.

Never make the mistake of thinking that you only need to socialize a young puppy and then they will be fine for the rest of their life, as all dogs require constant socializing and once they reach adolescence, their personality can really begin to assert itself.

Chapter Six: Training and Behavior Modification

All dogs need to be exposed to different people, dogs, places and unusual sights and sounds when they are puppies and throughout their adult life.

Any dog that is not regularly socialized may become shy or suspicious of unfamiliar or unusual people or circumstances, which could lead to nervous or fearful behavior, which can then lead to aggression.

1. With Other Dogs and Pets

Generally speaking, the majority of an adult dog's habits and behavioral traits will be formed between the ages of birth and one year of age.

This is why it will be very important to introduce your puppy to a wide variety of locations, sights, sounds, smells and situations during the most formative period in their young life, which is usually the first 16 weeks.

Your puppy will learn how to behave in all these various circumstances by following your lead, feeling your energy and watching how you react in every situation.

For instance, never accidentally reward your puppy or dog for displaying nervousness, fear or growling at another dog or person by picking them up.

Picking up a puppy or dog at a time when they are displaying unbalanced energy actually turns out to be a

Chapter Six: Training and Behavior Modification

reward for them, and you will be teaching them to continue with this type of behavior.

Picking up a puppy places them in a top dog position, where they have the higher ground and literally (because they are higher up) become more dominant than the person or dog they may have just growled at.

The correct action to take in such a situation is to gently correct your puppy with a firm yet calm energy by distracting them with a "no", or a quick sideways snap of the leash to get their attention back on you, so that they learn to let you deal with the situation on their behalf.

If you allow a fearful, nervous or shy puppy deal with situations that unnerve them without your direction, they may learn to react with fear or aggression to unfamiliar circumstances and you will have created a problem that could escalate into something more serious as they grow older.

The same is true of situations where a young puppy may feel the need to protect itself from a larger or older dog that may come charging in for a sniff. It is the guardian's responsibility to protect the puppy so that they do not feel that they must react with fear or aggression in order to protect themselves.

Once your puppy has received all their vaccinations, you can take them out to public dog parks and various locations where many dogs and people are found.

Before allowing them to interact with other dogs or puppies, take them for a disciplined walk on leash so that they

Chapter Six: Training and Behavior Modification

will be a little tired and less likely to immediately pounce excitedly on all other dogs.

Keep your puppy on leash and close beside you, because most young puppies are a bundle of out of control energy, and you need to protect them while teaching them how far they can go before they may get themselves into trouble with adult dogs that might not appreciate their excited playfulness.

Remember that they may not have experienced the company of other dogs since you brought them home, and now that they have completed their course of vaccinations, they will understandably be excited and perhaps a little hesitant about seeing dogs again.

Keep a close watch on your Vizsla puppy to make sure they are not being overwhelmed by too many other dogs, or getting overly excited and stressed or nervous, because it is your job to protect your puppy.

If your puppy shows any signs of aggression or domination toward another puppy, dog or person, you must immediately step in and calmly discipline them, otherwise by doing nothing you will be agreeing with their behavior and will be allowing them to get into situations that could become serious behavioral issues as they grow in age and size.

No matter the age or size of your puppy, allowing them to display aggression or domination over another dog or person is never a laughing matter and this type of behavior must be immediately curtailed.

Chapter Six: Training and Behavior Modification

2. With Other People

Take your puppy everywhere with you and introduce them to many different people of all ages, sizes and ethnicities so they will learn what is normal. This will be easy to do, because most people will automatically be drawn to you when they see you have a puppy.

Most humans will want to interact with your puppy and if they ask to hold your puppy this is a good opportunity to socialize your puppy and show them that humans are friendly.

Do not let others (especially young children) play roughly with your puppy or squeal at them in a high-pitched voices because this can be very frightening for a young puppy. You do not want to teach your puppy that humans are a source of crazy, excited energy.

Be especially careful when introducing your puppy to young children who may accidentally hurt your puppy, because you don't want your dog to become fearful of children as this could lead to aggression issues later on in life.

Explain to children that your puppy is very young and that they must be calm and gentle when playing or interacting in any way.

Chapter Six: Training and Behavior Modification

3. Within Different Environments

It can be a big mistake not to take the time to introduce your puppy to a wide variety of different environments because when they are not comfortable with different sights and sounds, this could cause them possible trauma later in their adult life.

Be creative and take your puppy everywhere you can imagine when they are young so that no matter where they travel, whether strolling along a noisy city sidewalk or beside a peaceful shoreline, they will be equally comfortable.

Do not make the mistake of only taking your puppy into areas where you live and will always travel because they need to also be comfortable visiting areas you might not often visit, such as noisy construction sites, airports or a shopping area across town. Your puppy needs to see all sorts of sights, sounds and situations so that they will not become fearful should they need to travel with you to any of these areas.

Your puppy will take their cues from you, which means that when you are calm and in control of every situation, they will learn to be the same because they will trust your lead. For instance, take them to the airport where they can watch people and hear planes landing and taking off or take them to a local park where they can see a baseball game, or for a stroll beside a schoolyard at recess time when noisy children are out playing, or take them to the local zoo or farm and let them get a close up look at horses, pigs and ducks.

Chapter Six: Training and Behavior Modification

Again, never think that socialization is something that only takes place when your dog is a young puppy, as proper socialization is ongoing for your dog's entire life.

4. Loud Noises

Many dogs can show extreme fear of loud noises, such as fireworks or thunderstorms.

When you take the time to desensitize your dog to these types of noises when they are very young, it will be much easier on them during stormy weather or holidays such as Halloween or New Year's when fireworks are often a part of the festivities. You can purchase CD's that are a collection of unusual sounds, such as vacuums or hoovers, airplanes, sirens, smoke alarms, fireworks, people clapping hands, screaming children, and more (or you can easily make your own), that you can play while working in your kitchen or relaxing in your living room or lounge. When you play these sounds and pretend that everything is normal, the next time your puppy or dog hears these types of sounds elsewhere, they will not become upset or agitated because they have learned to ignore them.

TIP: bubble wrap is also another simple way to desensitize a dog that is fearful of popping sounds. Show them the bubble wrap, pop a few of the cells and if they do not run away, give them a treat. You can start with the bubble wrap that has small, quieter cells, and then graduate them to the larger celled (louder) bubble wrap.

Chapter Six: Training and Behavior Modification

Also make sure that you get your young puppy used to the sounds of thunder and fireworks at an early age because these types of shrieking, crashing, banging and popping sounds of fireworks or thunder as well as the high-pitched beeping of household smoke and fire alarms can be so traumatic and unsettling for many dogs, that sometimes, no matter how much you try to calm your dog or pretend that everything is fine, there is little you can do.

Some dogs literally lose their minds when they hear the loud popping or screeching noises of fireworks and alarms and start trembling, running or trying to hide and you cannot communicate with them at all.

Make sure that your dog cannot harm itself trying to escape from these types of noises, and if possible, hold them until they begin to relax.

If your dog loses its mind when it hears these types of noises, simply avoid taking them anywhere near fireworks and if at times when they might hear these noises going off outside, play your inside music or TV louder than you might normally, to help disguise the exterior noise of fireworks or thunder.

Some dogs will respond well to wearing a "ThunderShirt", which is specifically designed to alleviate anxiety or trauma associated with loud rumbling, popping or banging noises.

Chapter Six: Training and Behavior Modification

The idea behind the design of the ThunderShirt is that the gentle pressure it creates is similar to a hug that, for some dogs, has a calming effect.

Do not underestimate the importance of taking the time to continually (not just when they are puppies) socialize and desensitize your puppy to all manner of sights, sounds, individuals and locations because to do so will be teaching them to be a calm and well-balanced member of your family that will quietly follow you in every situation.

Chapter Six: Training and Behavior Modification

Chapter Seven: Vet Care for Your Vizsla Dog

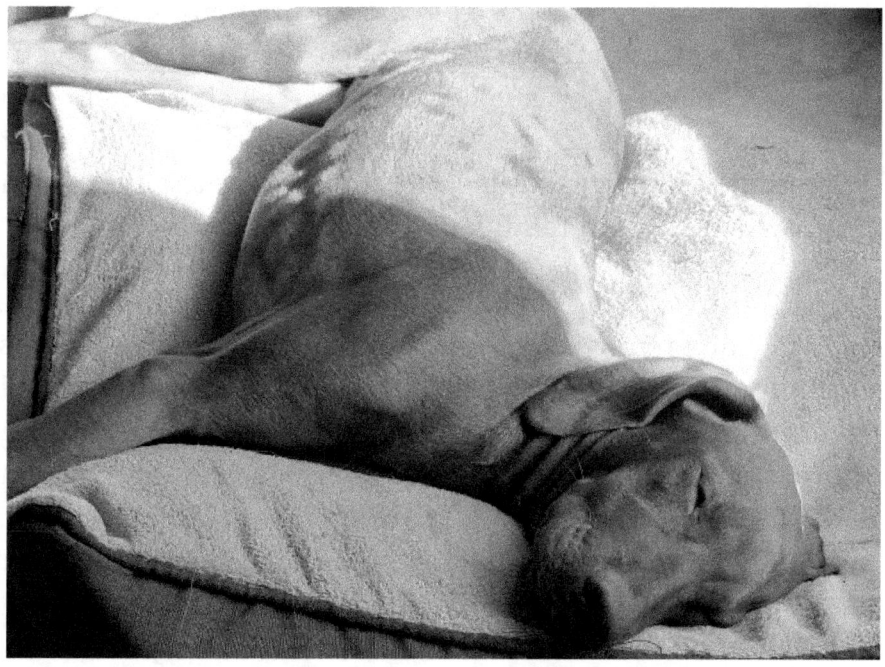

Vizsla's good health is largely dependent on you. Your veterinarian can recommend vaccinations, diet, and routine health care, but without your cooperation, your Vizsla will not be at the peak of health. Educate yourself on what is normal and abnormal with a dog. Learn the warning signs of major illnesses. You will be able to communicate more effectively with your veterinarian, and your attentiveness may someday save your dog's life.

Chapter Seven: Vet Care for Your Vizsla Dog

Spaying and Neutering

Unless you're new to dog ownership, you've probably heard someone talk about spaying and neutering your pet. Maybe it was the breeder from whom you purchased your Vizsla or maybe it was a worker in the shelter where you found your Vizsla. If you haven't planned on spaying or neutering your dog, and he is a pet that you are never going to show, you should rethink your decision.

With spaying and neutering, a pet's reproductive organs are removed. There are many health benefits including the elimination or reduction of certain cancers and tumors. Contrary to common belief, spaying or neutering doesn't make your Vizsla fat, though you may have to cut back a bit on feeding him. It also doesn't ruin his personality. In fact, with most dogs, spaying or neutering improves your dog's personality and attentiveness.

But, if you're like many purebred owners, you may be thinking that because your Vizsla is purebred, you should keep him intact and maybe breed him. This is not a good idea, for several reasons:

1. Most Vizsla dogs sold to pet homes are pet quality, at best. By breeding a pet-quality Vizsla, you're breeding mediocre puppies and contributing to the pet overpopulation.
2. Although you might have paid a lot for your Vizsla, adult purebred pet-quality dogs aren't worth a lot in the pet marketplace. Purebred rescue and shelters have adoption fees to

Chapter Seven: Vet Care for Your Vizsla Dog

ensure that they place the dog in a serious home and not with a wholesaler who will sell the dog to research facilities.

3. You will have to spend hundreds, if not thousands, of dollars to prove your Vizsla clear of hereditary diseases.
4. If you don't spay or neuter, you must be careful enough to prevent another dog from jumping into your backyard and mating with your Vizsla (or to keep your Vizsla from jumping out). Accidents happen all the time.
5. You run the risk of not being able to sell the puppies. How is your Vizsla more special than other dogs? Does he have Schutzhund, conformation, agility, herding, or obedience titles? Why would anyone want to buy your puppies when there are hundreds of other sellers?
6. You must be willing to be responsible and screen buyers and take back every Vizsla you've bred.
7. You could lose your Vizsla female if she has problems during whelping. Puppies are born dead or malformed all the time. There may be a blockage that requires veterinary intervention. Even then, whelping pups is a risky business.

Chapter Seven: Vet Care for Your Vizsla Dog

Vaccinations

Your Vizsla needs to be vaccinated against deadly and contagious diseases such as rabies, distemper, parvovirus, and canine hepatitis to ensure his health. Diseases such as parvovirus and distemper have a mortality rate of over 50 percent.

But what vaccinations are really necessary? Over the years, new data suggests that we overvaccinate our dogs, causing autoimmune disorders and other health problems. But failing to vaccinate may cause disease to spread. It is a tough decision and one you should make with your veterinarian. Your vet should recommend vaccinations according to your location and your Vizsla's exposure to other dogs and canids.

Vaccines work by introducing a small amount of the disease-causing organism into a healthy dog. The dog's immune system responds by producing antibodies that are then ready to fight any subsequent infections. Sick dogs or dogs with poor immune systems should not be vaccinated without a veterinarian's approval. There are three types of vaccines available: modified live, killed, and recombinant. Modified live vaccines are genetically engineered versions of the organism's more deadly form. Modified live viruses and bacteria are able to reproduce, but they generally do no harm to a healthy dog. The dog's body produces more antibodies to fight the infection as the modified live organism reproduces. Killed vaccines are based on the killed form of the organism. Killed vaccines do not reproduce in the dog and usually cause the body to produce fewer antibodies than the live versions.

Chapter Seven: Vet Care for Your Vizsla Dog

Recombinant vaccines are genetically engineered vaccines where either the virulent genes of the disease are removed or the genetic material of the disease is added to a carrier disease that will infect the dog and produce an immune response.

Performing Health Check

Perform regular health checks while your Vizsla is healthy so that you can identify any abnormalities quickly. A routine health check will help you monitor your dog's overall condition and determine whether a trip to the veterinarian is due. While most veterinarians perform health checks with annual vaccinations, once a year may not be enough to catch sudden conditions.

Perform a health check on your Vizsla at least once a week. A good time to do this is while you're grooming him. If you find something that feels strange, try feeling for it on the opposite side. Normal features are usually symmetrical. If you are unsure of what is normal, ask your veterinarian. She can show you what looks and feels correct.

Checking the Head

The eyes should be clear and bright with no signs of redness. There should be no excessive discharge. There should be no yellow or pus-like discharge. Dogs do not cry, so any tears may suggest foreign bodies or irritation.

Chapter Seven: Vet Care for Your Vizsla Dog

The nose should be cool and wet to the touch. There should be no discharge. A dry and hot nose may indicate fever. Also, your Vizsla should not be sneezing constantly.

The ears should be clean and free of waxy buildup. Smell the ear. Does it smell clean or bad? Dark red or black buildup may indicate an infection or the presence of mites.

The gums should be pink and clean, not red and swollen, and the teeth should be white. Look for broken teeth and teeth that have not come in properly. If your Vizsla is over six months old, he should not have any puppy teeth. The tongue should be pink, and your Vizsla's breath should not smell bad. If it does, it may signal an underlying health problem such as gum disease.

Checking the Body

Feel down each leg. You should feel no unusual lumps or bumps. If you find a lump, check the other leg to see if the feature is symmetrical. Elbows, pads, and dewclaws can be accidentally mistaken for tumors or bumps, so if in doubt look at the lump. Move the leg slowly in its full range of motion. The movement should be fluid. If your Vizsla shows distress, or if there are any clicks, grinding, or catches, these may signal arthritis or joint problems.

Inspect the feet, both top and bottom. The skin around the toenail should be healthy, not red. The toenails should not be broken or too long. There should be no redness to the fur

Chapter Seven: Vet Care for Your Vizsla Dog

around the toes. If there is, your Vizsla might be licking his toes due to allergies or foreign bodies. Check the pads and in between the toes for cracks, splits, and foreign objects.

Feel along the back and ribs. You should be able to feel the spine and ribs easily. If you are unable to, your Vizsla may be overweight. He should show no sensitivity to touch along the back and the area where the kidneys are. Feel for lumps along the side. If your Vizsla hunches his back or shows sensitivity, it may indicate a more serious problem. His belly should be clean and free from dirt. Look for flea droppings and other parasites.

How to Take Your Dog's Temperature

Use an electronic thermometer that can also be used rectally. Wash the thermometer with soapy water and sterilize it with isopropyl alcohol. Use petroleum jelly as a lubricant and gently insert the thermometer into your Vizsla's rectum. Hold him quietly for about two minutes to obtain a reading. Do not allow him to sit down to keep from breaking the thermometer or pushing it farther into his rectum. Normal temperatures for Vizsla dogs are 100.5°F to 102°F. (There are now ear thermometers for dogs that work on the same principle as the ear thermometers for humans.)

Chapter Seven: Vet Care for Your Vizsla Dog

Common Illnesses and Injuries

Vizslas are big, active dogs, but sometimes an injury or illness can lay them low. Most dogs at some point will itch and scratch from allergies, hot spots, or flea bites, suffer the unpleasantness of diarrhea or vomiting, or develop lumps or bumps that should be checked out. Being the outdoor athletes that they are, Vizslas are also prone to such injuries as broken toenails, cuts and scrapes, or ruptured cruciate ligaments. Knowing what to expect and what to do about these potential problems will help you recognize and deal with them when they occur.

When Do You Need to Visit the Vet?

Every dog should be examined annually by a veterinarian. Even if you choose not to vaccinate your Vizsla every year, he still needs a physical exam to make sure his overall health is good. During this physical exam, the vet will listen to the dog's heart and lungs; take his temperature, pulse, and breathing rate; weigh him; check the eyes, ears, and skin for infection or parasites; look inside the mouth to make sure there's no tartar buildup on teeth or other dental problems; test his range of motion to make sure his movement is smooth (not stiff); and palpate (feel) his body to make sure the organs don't seem enlarged and that there are no suspicious lumps or bumps that could indicate infections or tumors.

Besides this annual exam, your Vizsla should go to the veterinarian any time he has a serious injury or illness. A small cut or scrape can usually be treated at home, and minor

Chapter Seven: Vet Care for Your Vizsla Dog

bouts of vomiting or diarrhea usually aren't a problem. A visit to the veterinarian is warranted if vomiting or diarrhea is frequent or lasts for more than forty-eight hours, if the dog's behavior is unusual — say, lack of appetite for more than a day — or if the dog suffers an injury that causes lameness or that you can't treat with your canine first-aid kit. Following are some examples of the common illnesses or injuries that your Vizsla might encounter and what to do about them.

The annual exam is also a good time to take in a fecal sample to make sure your Vizsla doesn't have any intestinal parasites.

Allergies

An allergy is a reaction of the immune system. It's caused by exposure to an allergen, which is any substance — medications, insect bites or stings, grasses, pollens, molds, and foods — capable of causing an allergic reaction. Dogs can inherit allergic tendencies or acquire allergies, and it's estimated that one in seven dogs suffers from some type of allergy.

Allergic Skin Disease

Vizslas are among the breeds that are prone to allergic skin disease. It usually appears when a dog is young — one to three years old. Atopy, which is usually an inherited tendency, is characterized by an itch-scratch cycle that's usually triggered by pollens. Eventually, the dog may begin reacting to all kinds of allergens, from dust and feathers to molds and wool.

Dogs with atopy itch and scratch constantly, resulting in hair loss and scabbing. The skin becomes thick and flaky. It's also not unusual for dogs with atopy to develop other infections that develop as a result of the wounds caused by scratching.

It takes lots of testing to determine whether a dog is suffering from allergic skin disease or some other type of allergy. The veterinarian may order skin scrapings, bacterial and fungal cultures, intradermal skin testing (which involves injecting tiny amounts of known allergens and observing the skin reaction), and even a trial period on a special diet. A good flea-control plan is also important, because FAD can resemble atopy.

Once atopy is diagnosed, there are several ways to manage it. The first is to change the dog's environment — as much as possible — by limiting exposure to known allergens. Antihistamines, essential fatty acid (EFA) supplements, and medicated shampoos can help control itching and scratching. A Vizsla that suffers severe itching may need intermittent low doses of corticosteroids to relieve itching. When all else fails, allergy shots (hyposensitization) can be given. This involves skin testing (to identify specific allergens) and then desensitizing the dog to these irritants through a series of injections.

Atopy usually starts out as a seasonal condition but can become a year-round problem if the dog develops multiple allergies to common household or environmental substances, such as wool or house dust.

Chapter Seven: Vet Care for Your Vizsla Dog

Flea Allergy Dermatitis (FAD)

A single bite from a single flea can trigger flea-allergy dermatitis, which is the most common allergy seen in dogs. The allergy occurs because many dogs are sensitive to a particular substance in flea saliva. Dogs with FAD itch like crazy, and their skin is inflamed, red, and bumpy. Depending on where you live, FAD can be seasonal or year-round.

The best treatment for FAD is a good flea-control program, so talk to your veterinarian about appropriate products to use. Until fleas are under control, itching can be controlled with antihistamines and — if necessary — short term doses of corticosteroids. Some dogs develop skin infections from chewing at the itchy spots. These can be cleared up with topical (on the skin) and oral (taken by mouth) antibiotics.

Food Allergies

Signs of food allergies are severe itching and red, bumpy, or raised patches of skin. This rash is usually seen on the ears, feet, stomach, and back of the legs. Wheat and corn are common food allergens.

Feeding your Vizsla a hypoallergenic food won't prevent allergies from developing. These foods contain unusual proteins that most dogs haven't been exposed to,

Chapter Seven: Vet Care for Your Vizsla Dog

which makes it easier to figure out which ingredients are causing the problem.

When a food allergy is suspected, the veterinarian will recommend putting the dog on a hypoallergenic diet for a certain period of time — usually six to ten weeks. A hypoallergenic diet contains unusual ingredients — catfish and potatoes, for instance — that the dog has likely not encountered before. It's also free of artificial colors, flavors, and preservatives. If the food allergy goes away while the dog is on a hypoallergenic diet, it's necessary to add ingredients back to the diet until the allergenic culprit is identified. Then a homemade or commercial diet can be chosen that doesn't contain the allergy-causing ingredient(s).

Contact Allergies

This type of allergy occurs when a dog comes in contact with a substance that irritates the skin. Common items that contain such irritating substances are soaps and shampoos, plastic or rubber dishes, flea collars, wool or synthetic fibers, and topical medications containing neomycin. If your Vizsla develops skin irritation on the nose or lips (plastic or rubber dish allergy), irritation or hair loss around the neck (flea collar), or irritation on the feet, legs, and stomach, suspect a contact allergy. Try to identify and remove the offending substance. In the meantime, your veterinarian can prescribe medication to help relieve the itching.

What Are Hot Spots?

Chapter Seven: Vet Care for Your Vizsla Dog

These warm, painful, swollen patches of skin usually develop in response to flea bites, allergies, other skin diseases, or lack of grooming (when dead hair gets trapped against the skin). If your Vizsla gets a hot spot, clip away the hair and clean the skin with chlorhexidine. Severe or numerous hot spots may require a trip to the veterinarian so the dog can be sedated or anesthetized during this procedure. Your veterinarian can also prescribe medication to relieve the itching until the hot spot clears up. Your Vizsla may need to wear a cone-shaped Elizabethan collar to prevent him from biting or scratching at the area.

Cuts, Scrapes, and Foxtails

There are all kinds of ways that active Vizslas can acquire cuts, scrapes, or foxtails. For cuts and scrapes, simply clean it with chlorhexidine (Nolvasan), available from your drugstore — unless the wound is deep and requires stitches. (Hydrogen peroxide is out of favor as a wound cleanser because it can cause cellular damage.) Then apply an antibiotic ointment (also available from the drug-store) to help prevent infection. Check the injured area regularly to make sure it's healing nicely and doesn't need veterinary attention. Signs of infection are redness, tenderness, and swelling.

A foxtail is a type of grass with spikes that resembles brushes. Dogs that spend time outdoors — the average Vizsla, for instance — will most likely encounter foxtails at some point. The grassy heads start to dry in the spring and are most likely to cause problems in summer and early fall. With their sharp ends and microscopic barbs along the sides, foxtails can become embedded in your Vizsla's eyes, ears, nose, paws, and fur. They can work themselves into the body, causing infection and even death if they migrate to the brain, heart, lungs, or spinal cord.

If you live in an area where foxtails are common, check your Vizsla for them after every excursion outdoors. Remove any that are clinging to the surface of your Vizsla's coat or that are outside the ear canal. It may help to soften the foxtail first with mineral oil, vegetable oil, or baby oil. Suspect a foxtail in the ear, eye, nose, or paw if your Vizsla is shaking his head or pawing at his ears; if he's squinting or his eye appears "glued" shut; if he begins sneezing repetitively or sneezes blood; or if he constantly licks his paw or it appears swollen.

Trying to remove a foxtail from the ear can push it in further, and foxtails can't be flushed from the eye with water or saline solution. Take your Vizsla to the vet to have these removed.

Diarrhea, Vomiting, and Lack of Appetite

If your Vizsla's stools appear loose or liquid instead of firm and compact, he has diarrhea. Diarrhea has many causes, ranging from eating something that doesn't agree with the dog's digestive system to intestinal parasites to excitement or anxiety. Some infectious or chronic diseases may also cause diarrhea. Depending on the signs, diarrhea may or may not require a veterinary visit.

Chapter Seven: Vet Care for Your Vizsla Dog

If you suspect that your Vizsla's diarrhea results from anxiety or excitement, or because he stole some spicy or fatty food and is suffering the consequences, withhold food for twenty-four hours, but make sure he has plenty of water to drink — diarrhea can cause dehydration. For the next couple of days, you can feed him a bland diet of skinless boiled chicken with white rice, or cottage cheese. Other easily digestible foods you can give are boiled hamburger meat, cooked macaroni, and soft-boiled eggs. Gradually replace the bland diet with his regular food. If diarrhea continues for more than twenty-four hours, take the dog to the veterinarian. Diarrhea that's bloody, black, or tarry looking or that's accompanied by vomiting, weakness, or fever calls for an immediate veterinary visit.

It's not unusual for Vizslas to eat gravel or even rocks. If your Vizsla starts throwing up gravel or has intermittent vomiting and diarrhea, an intestinal obstruction may be the problem. Surgery may be necessary for large objects such as rocks, but if your dog eats gravel your veterinarian may suggest dosing him with mineral oil for a week to clear out the tiny stones.

Like diarrhea, vomiting can be caused by any number of problems, including anxiety or excitement, eating too quickly, or eating something that doesn't agree with the digestive system. Vomiting is also a sign of some infectious or chronic diseases. If your Vizsla is healthy and you suspect the vomiting is related to eating something that didn't agree with him, withhold food and water for twelve hours, then feed a bland meal, such as boiled chicken and rice. Give only one or

Chapter Seven: Vet Care for Your Vizsla Dog

two tablespoons at first to make sure your dog can keep the food down. If he can, gradually return him to his regular diet. Take your Vizsla to the vet if he has projectile (violent) vomiting, if the vomit smells like feces, if the vomiting is accompanied by diarrhea, if the vomiting continues even though the dog hasn't had any food, or if the vomit contains blood or worms.

Vizslas love to eat, so a consistent lack of appetite is cause for concern. Not wanting to eat can have any number of causes, from poor dental health (when it hurts to chew) to viral diseases, such as distemper or infectious canine hepatitis. Any time your Vizsla loses interest in food — especially if appetite loss is accompanied by lethargy or other signs of problems — take him to the veterinarian.

Lumps and Bumps

Dogs can develop all kinds of lumps and bumps on or beneath the skin. Some are harmless while others require veterinary intervention. Look (and feel) for lumps and bumps whenever you groom your Vizsla.

Abscesses, Hematomas, and Adenomas

A soft, painful lump may be an abscess or hematoma. An abscess is an infected area caused by a bite or puncture wound, whereas a hematoma is a blood clot beneath the skin. Ear hematomas are common in dogs. Abscesses must be drained by the veterinarian and treated with antibiotics, whereas some hematomas disappear on their own — if they don't they must also be drained by the veterinarian.

Some lumps look like small, smooth, pink warts and appear on the eyelids or legs. These benign (harmless) tumors are sebaceous adenomas and are commonly seen in older dogs. Tumors on the eyelids should be removed to prevent damage to the cornea.

Ceruminous (wax-producing) gland adenomas can develop in the ear canal. They're a pinkish-white color and dome-shaped. Sometimes they become ulcerated or infected. Small tumors of this type are usually harmless, but large ones can become invasive and must be treated with surgery and radiation therapy.

Warts and Cysts

Papillomas (warts) are caused by a virus and can grow on the skin or inside the mouth. They are usually harmless and don't need to be removed unless they're causing a problem because of their location on the body.

Cysts are firm lumps beneath the skin. They form when hair follicles become blocked with hair and a cheesy material called sebum. Cysts are generally harmless, but they can become infected and may need to be drained surgically or removed.

Skin melanomas are usually harmless, but melanomas in the mouth and nail bed are usually malignant. They should be removed surgically, but they often recur. Dogs with melanomas in the mouth don't have a good prognosis.

Skin Cancer

Dogs can develop several different types of skin cancer: basal cell tumors, mast cell tumors, melanomas, and squamous cell carcinomas. Fortunately, none of these conditions are especially common in Vizslas.

Basal cell tumors are common, usually occurring on the head and neck. They feel firm and have distinct borders. Surgical removal is the best treatment. Mast cell tumors make up 10 to 20 percent of the skin tumors seen in dogs. They have many nodules and usually look red, hairless, and ulcerated. Mast cell tumors can be either benign (harmless) or malignant (harmful) and should be removed surgically. Dogs with malignant mast cell tumors may also need radiation or chemotherapy.

Melanomas develop from cells in the skin that produce melanin, which is what gives your Vizsla the dark pigment on his nose and skin. Melanomas look like brown or black nodules and can occur on the eyelids, lips, in the mouth, on the nail beds, and elsewhere on the body.

Squamous cell carcinomas are caused by exposure to the ultraviolet radiation in sunlight. They're usually found on lightly pigmented areas of the body. Appearance ranges from a firm red patch to a cauliflowerlike growth to a hard, flat, grayish-looking ulcer that doesn't heal. They can be removed surgically or treated with radiation therapy if surgery isn't possible.

Tumors

Other lumps that you might find on your Vizsla are perianal gland tumors or venereal tumors. Perianal gland tumors are solitary or multinodular growths around the anal area and occur in older males that haven't been neutered. The tumors are removed surgically, and the dog is neutered. Radiation and chemotherapy may be necessary for malignant tumors.

Venereal tumors, which can resemble cauliflower or single nodules on a stalk, are unusual. They're spread sexually or by licking, biting, or scratching. Chemotherapy is the usual treatment, and spaying or neutering is recommended as well.

Orthopedic Problems

Musculoskeletal problems, which affect the bones, joints, and muscles, are common in dogs, and Vizslas are no exception. As a breed, they are prone to hip and elbow dysplasia and osteochondritis dissecans. Other problems that can occur include ruptured cruciated ligament and toe injuries.

If your veterinarian determines that your puppy has unusually loose hip joints, you may want to look into a surgical technique to close the area between the two halves of the pelvis. The surgery must be performed before five months of age, so the pup must be evaluated early.

Hip Dysplasia

Hip dysplasia occurs when the head of the thigh bone (femur) doesn't fit properly into the hip socket, causing joint laxity (looseness), inflammation, pain, and lameness. Signs of hip dysplasia include limping and a lack of enthusiasm for exercise — very unusual in an active Vizsla puppy! An x-ray of the hips and pelvis can confirm whether there's a problem. In mild cases, nutraceuticals, such as glucosamine and chondroitin, and pain-relieving medications, can help a Vizsla get along. When hip dysplasia is severe, though, total hip replacement is the best treatment.

Elbow Dysplasia

Elbow dysplasia is caused by the failure of the elbow bones of one or both forelegs to unite and move properly, or by bone fragments within the joint. Lameness is the primary sign of elbow dysplasia, and the problem can be confirmed with x-rays. Like hip dysplasia, it can often be managed with nutraceuticals and anti-inflammatory medications. Exercise, such as swimming and walks on leash, can help maintain the range of joint motion and strengthen the surrounding muscles, improving joint stability and the health of the joint fluid. Severe elbow dysplasia may require surgery to fuse the joint and relieve the pain.

Osteochondritis Dissecans (OCD)

Osteochondritis dissecans (OCD) is a problem of cartilage development that usually affects shoulder joints but can also affect the elbow, hocks, and stifles (knees). Vizslas with OCD may gradually become lame or show pain when the affected joint is flexed or extended. X-rays provide a definitive diagnosis. The recommended treatment for OCD is rest and joint-protective nutraceuticals to help prevent pain, inflammation, and further degeneration. If the elbow or shoulder joints are affected, your veterinarian may advise surgery to scrape away defective cartilage or remove cartilage flaps loose in the joint.

Ruptured Cruciate Ligament

Also known as an anterior cruciate ligament (ACL) tear, this is a common injury in retrievers. It usually occurs when the knee twists suddenly or hyperextends. ACL tears are one of the major causes of arthritis in the canine knee joint. If your Vizsla suffers an ACL tear, you'll know. He'll hold up the injured leg or cry out. The knee joint will be swollen and painful. A surgical procedure called tibial plateau leveling osteotomy (TPLO) is the best treatment.

If an ACL tear occurs in one knee, the ligament in the other knee is likely to tear at some time in the future.

Toe Injuries

Active dogs are likely to suffer toe injuries at some point. These can range from a broken toenail to a dislocated or sprained toe. Toes can become broken, dislocated (rupture of ligaments), or sprained (rupture of tendons) if the dog bangs the toe hard against something, steps in a hole, or lands wrong from a jump. A toe injury might be the problem if your Vizsla is limping.

Sometimes toes heal on their own, but surgery may be necessary to repair the structure. Run any toe injuries by your veterinarian to make sure they're not serious. An x-ray can find slight fractures that might otherwise be missed.

When nails are kept short, broken toenails are unlikely. If your Vizsla does break a toenail while running or by snagging it on carpet fibers, the injury is likely to bleed profusely. It looks scary, but you can stop the bleeding by putting pressure on the wound with a cloth or towel until the bleeding stops. If the toenail doesn't break off cleanly, it's a good idea to take the dog to the veterinarian to have it removed. Removal can be painful and may require anesthesia. Usually, the toenail will grow back.

Eye Diseases

Common eye diseases in Vizslas are retinal dysplasia, cataracts, and progressive retinal atrophy. These hereditary problems can be screened for before dogs are bred. Ask the breeder for documentation from the Canine Eye Registry Foundation (CERF) that your pup's parents are free of these conditions.

Chapter Seven: Vet Care for Your Vizsla Dog

The term retinal dysplasia applies to a number of conditions in which the retina doesn't develop properly. Some are acquired, while others are hereditary, and Vizslas are among the breeds in which inherited retinal dysplasias are found. It's sometimes the case that Vizslas with skeletal abnormalities also have retinal dysplasia, and it may be that the same gene causes both problems. Signs of retinal dysplasia range from lines or curves on the back part of the eye — known as retinal folds — to generalized retinal detachment. Some dogs with retinal dysplasia have little visual loss, but blindness results if the retina detaches.

Researchers at the University of California at Davis Institute of Genetic Disease Control have established a registry for Labradors diagnosed with tricuspid valve dysplasia (TVD), so they can track the disease's prevalence and mode of inheritance in the breed. Ask the breeder if your pup's parents have been screened by echocardiogram to be free of TVD.

A cataract is an opaque spot on the eye's lens, which is normally clear. Cataracts can be acquired as a consequence of aging or are inherited, and can eventually lead to vision loss. Vizslas are one of the breeds in which congenital, or juvenile, cataracts have been documented. With their great sense of smell, Vizslas can get around just fine without their eyesight, but if necessary, cataracts can be removed surgically.

Progressive retinal atrophy (PRA) is an inherited degeneration of the retina that results in lowered vision or blindness. Signs of PRA are fear of the dark and obvious night blindness. This eye disease has no treatment or cure, although genetic research is promising. The best way to prevent PRA is to breed only Vizslas that are certified free of PRA.

Tricuspid Valve Dysplasia (TVD)

This congenital (meaning it's present from birth) heart disorder is increasingly common in Vizslas, and it is believed to be inherited. A deformity of the heart's tricuspid valve causes abnormal blood flow and increases the workload of the right side of the heart. Eventually, the dog suffers congestive heart failure. Signs of TVD include a heart murmur or lack of energy. An echocardiogram (ultrasound) is the best way to diagnose TVD, but electrocardiography (EKG) or x-rays may also be used.

Unfortunately, there's no treatment or cure for TVD. Drugs can be given to control fluid retention and help regulate the heart, but the life expectancy for a dog with TVD is only one to three years. Sometimes dogs don't show signs until congestive heart failure occurs.

Epilepsy

Epilepsy is a brain disorder that causes recurrent seizures — convulsions that are set off by abnormal bursts of electrical activity in the brain. It's one of the most common neurologic diseases in dogs, and some forms are heritable. Inherited epilepsy is referred to as idiopathic, meaning the

Chapter Seven: Vet Care for Your Vizsla Dog

cause is unknown. Vizslas are one of the breeds prone to idiopathic epilepsy.

The length of epileptic seizures can range from a few seconds to a few minutes. In rare cases, they can continue for an hour or more. Mild forms of epilepsy can be treated with medication to control the seizures. There's no screening test for epilepsy, and it often doesn't appear until a dog is older. The incidence of epilepsy can be reduced through selective breeding, however. The breeder should be able to tell you the frequency of epilepsy in his or her dogs.

Emergencies

The injuries and illnesses described in the previous section can be serious, but they're not emergencies. An emergency is a life-threatening situation. It's to be hoped that your Vizsla will never suffer an injury or illness that's an emergency, but it never hurts to be prepared. Knowing what to do for fractures, bites, choking, and other dangerous health circumstances will help you stay calm and give your Vizsla a better chance at survival.

First-Aid Kit

A first-aid kit for dogs is much like one for humans. You can probably use the same one you keep on hand for your family, or you can put together a separate one for your Vizsla.

Chapter Seven: Vet Care for Your Vizsla Dog

Keep the first-aid kit in your bathroom or on top of your dog's crate, so it's easily accessible when you need it. Make sure everyone in the family knows where the first-aid kit is in case you may need to send one of them to find it some day. The following items, available from drugstores, should be part of any well-stocked first-aid kit:

- Ace bandage
- Adhesive tape
- Antibiotic ointment
- Blunt scissors
- Gauze pads and rolls
- Muzzle
- Needle-nose pliers
- Compressed activated charcoal
- Cotton balls
- Cotton-tip applicators
- Disinfectant, such as chlorhexidine (Nolvasan) or povidone iodine (Betadine)
- Eye dropper
- Petroleum jelly
- Rectal thermometer (bulb or digital)

- Rubbing alcohol

- Sterile saline eye wash

- Surgical gloves

- Tweezers

Other useful items to have on hand are a blanket to keep the dog warm in case of shock, and clean towels or cloths for putting pressure on wounds that are bleeding. A penlight is helpful for examining eyes, mouth, and ears. Keep the phone numbers for your veterinarian's office, your veterinarian's on-call pager, the nearest animal emergency hospital, and a local or national poison-control center by your telephone or in the first-aid kit.

How to Muzzle Your Vizsla

When a dog is hurt and scared, he's liable to bite at anyone who tries to handle him, no matter how friendly he is normally or how much he loves the person trying to help him. A muzzle can keep your Vizsla from accidentally biting you, making it easier to care for him as needed. Before you try to examine him, put a muzzle on him, as a precaution for both of you.

Whatever muzzle you choose should be designed to allow the dog to breathe easily. It should be open at the end in case the dog throws up. Look for one with an adjustable-length strap and easy snap-in or Velcro fastener.

Muzzles can be made of cloth, nylon, or leather, and come in several different styles. Basket-style muzzles have a leather, wire, or plastic front that looks like a woven basket. A strap fastens the muzzle behind the dog's head. Some muzzles are made of fabric and are placed over the dog's nose and mouth, with a strap that goes around the head to hold it in place. Others fit around the nose and mouth with a strap that fastens behind the head. A soft cloth muzzle that fastens in the back with Velcro is probably easiest to use.

To put the muzzle on, kneel or stand at the dog's side rather than coming at it with the muzzle from the front. Slide the muzzle over the dog's nose and mouth and fasten it behind the head. If possible, have someone else hold the dog while you put the muzzle on. Speak soothingly during the process. It's a good idea to try the muzzle on your Vizsla before you need it so that it will already be properly adjusted for size if you need to put it on in a hurry.

Are there any times you shouldn't muzzle an injured dog? Yes. Never muzzle a dog that's unconscious or one that's coughing, vomiting, has a mouth injury, or is having difficulty breathing. And trying to put a muzzle on a dog that's actively resisting it by biting or snarling is not worth the risk of being bitten.

Does Your Vizsla Need CPR?

Cardiopulmonary resuscitation, or CPR, combines artificial respiration and heart massage. Artificial respiration is the act of breathing into a dog's nose to get the lungs going again when breathing has stopped. Heart massage is a series of chest compressions to help restart a heart that has stopped beating.

Before performing CPR, it's important to make sure the dog really needs it. Performing CPR on a dog that is still breathing or whose heart is beating can cause further injury. To check for breathing, see if the dog's chest is rising and falling — the chest movement may be very shallow. You can also hold a mirror to the dog's mouth to see if breath causes the mirror to fog.

Feel for a pulse to see if the heart is beating. Place your fingers on the femoral artery in the groin area (the inside of the hind leg). If the dog's heart is beating, you'll feel a pulse.

If the dog has a pulse but isn't breathing, perform artificial respiration. If the dog is breathing, but doesn't have a pulse, perform chest compressions. When the dog isn't breathing and doesn't have a pulse, you can perform CPR.

CPR is most effective when two people can work on the dog: one to perform rescue breathing and one to perform chest compressions. Emergencies that might call for the use of CPR include choking, electrical shock, or a traumatic injury that causes the heart and lungs to stop.

Rescue Breathing

Place your Vizsla on a flat surface, right side down. Open his mouth and pull his tongue forward. Wearing surgical gloves, swipe your fingers through the mouth to check for any foreign bodies and remove them if possible.

Place your hand around the muzzle to prevent air from escaping, and blow gently into the nose every two to three seconds. You should see the chest rise and fall. If you don't, blow more forcefully. Continue until the dog starts breathing again on his own, or until the heart stops beating.

Performing Chest Compressions

Position the dog in the same way as for rescue breathing. Kneel behind his back, and place the heel of one hand over the widest part of the rib cage (not over the heart).

Rest the heel of the other hand on top of the first. With elbows straight, push down firmly for one count, then release for one count. Try to perform eighty compressions per minute. If the dog's heart doesn't start beating within ten minutes, you're not likely to be successful.

Performing CPR

Position the dog in the same way as for rescue breathing or chest compressions. Give five compressions, followed by one breath. If you have another person helping you, give one breath after every two to three compressions. Continue for ten minutes or until the dog's breathing resumes and his pulse is steady, whichever comes first.

Never do CPR, chest compressions, or rescue breathing on a healthy dog "for practice." You could seriously injure him. Instead, sign up for one of the pet first-aid/CPR workshops offered by the American Red Cross.

How to Move an Injured Dog

As you probably learned at some point in your life, it can be dangerous to move a person with an injury. The same is true for dogs. If your Vizsla is injured and must be moved out of harm's way or transported to a veterinary hospital, you can take steps to minimize potential injuries from moving him.

If you must pick your dog up, keep the injured side away from your body. Lift him by placing one arm around his chest or between his front legs. Support his rear with your other arm. If a hind leg is injured, place your arm between the hind legs. Don't forget to bend your knees and lift with your legs; it's much easier on your back.

Another way to move the dog is to lay him on a blanket or a large, flat, sturdy piece of wood. This can then be used as a stretcher, but it will require two to four people to carry the dog (assuming it's a full-grown Vizsla). In the car, cushion the dog with pillows, towels, or rolled blankets. Keep him warm with a blanket or towel to help ward off shock.

Chapter Seven: Vet Care for Your Vizsla Dog

Dealing with Emergencies

Remember that an emergency is a life-threatening situation. The purpose of first aid is to keep the dog alive until he can receive veterinary help. By dealing with it quickly and calmly, you can greatly increase your Vizsla's chances of survival. Here's how to recognize some common emergencies and what to do for them.

Bleeding

No matter what kind of injury your Vizsla has, if he's bleeding, that's what should be dealt with first. Dogs can bleed to death in a matter of minutes if blood flow isn't controlled quickly. The first thing to determine is whether the bleeding is from an artery (bright red and spurting) or from a vein (darker red and slower flowing). Arterial bleeding is most serious, but in both cases, you need to put pressure on the wound and keep it there until bleeding stops.

Tourniquets can do more harm than good and should be used only as a last resort. Ask your veterinarian to show you how to apply one. Never use a tourniquet on any wound that can be controlled by direct pressure.

Using sterile gauze bandages (ideally) or in a pinch any type of cloth — from a towel to a T-shirt — apply firm, consistent pressure to the wound. It may take five to ten minutes for bleeding to stop completely.

Traumatic injuries, such as being hit by a car, and certain poisons can cause internal bleeding. Signs of internal

Chapter Seven: Vet Care for Your Vizsla Dog

bleeding are bleeding from the nose, mouth, or rectum; coughing blood; blood in urine; pale gums; and collapse. Keep your Vizsla warm and get him to the veterinarian as soon as possible.

Bloat

Sometimes referred to as gastric torsion or gastric dilatation volvulus, bloat occurs when the stomach fills up with gas and fluids and then twists. It's sort of like blowing up a balloon and tying it off. Bloat usually affects large, deep-chested dogs, including Vizslas.

You can help prevent bloat by feeding your Vizsla three times a day instead of once or twice. Restrict access to water immediately before and after meals, and limit the amount of water he drinks at one time. Strenuous exercise directly after eating can lead to bloat, so put your Vizsla in his crate for a nap after every meal.

The trapped gases and fluids cause abdominal pain, signaled by shallow breathing or a dull, vacant, or pained expression. The stomach looks stretched out and sounds hollow like a drum if thumped. Other signs of bloat include pacing restlessly, sluggish behavior, gagging, drooling, and unsuccessful attempts to throw up. Because the stomach is tied off, a dog with bloat is unable to vomit or belch. As the condition worsens, the pulse weakens, the gums become pale, and the dog collapses.

Bloat is not a condition where you want to take a wait-and-see attitude. If you even suspect it's a possibility, take your Vizsla to the veterinarian or to the emergency hospital if it's in the middle of the night. The earlier bloat is recognized and treated, the better chance your Vizsla has of surviving.

The veterinarian will pass a long plastic or rubber tube through the mouth and into the stomach, allowing air and fluid to escape. X-rays can determine whether the stomach is twisted, a condition that requires emergency surgery to return the stomach and spleen to their correct positions. Suturing the wall of the stomach to the abdominal wall helps prevent bloat from recurring.

Broken Bones

Your Vizsla might break a bone from a bad fall or from being hit by a car. Assume that a bone is broken if your Vizsla can't stand on a leg, if a bone is protruding through the skin, or if the dog can't move (a spinal injury, perhaps). Immediate veterinary care is a priority, but first you need to stabilize the dog.

After muzzling him for safety, pad a movable flat surface, such as a board or tarp with blankets or towels. Lay the dog on it and secure him so he doesn't fall off. If the break has caused an open wound, cover it with sterile gauze pads or a clean cloth, wrapping the cover loosely with a bandage to keep it on. Don't try to set a broken leg. It's most important to keep the dog warm and get him to a veterinarian quickly. After treatment, broken bones take eight to twelve weeks to heal.

Chapter Seven: Vet Care for Your Vizsla Dog

Choking

Your Vizsla can choke if something gets caught in his throat, such as a piece of rawhide. Suspect an obstruction if your Vizsla is pawing at his mouth, gagging or retching, or having difficulty breathing. If coughing doesn't dislodge the object and your Vizsla is conscious, get him to the veterinarian to have it removed. Trying to get your fingers around it to pull it out can push it further into the throat.

If your Vizsla loses consciousness because he can't breathe, lay him on his side, open his mouth, pull his tongue forward, and sweep your fingers through the mouth to see if you can grasp the object and remove it. Then perform rescue breathing or CPR if necessary. If it doesn't come out easily, move on to the Heimlich maneuver.

If the Heimlich maneuver doesn't work, try holding the dog's hind legs in the air and thumping his back between the shoulder blades with the heel of your hand. When the object is dislodged, perform rescue breathing or CPR as needed. Take the dog to the veterinarian for an exam to make sure he's okay.

To perform the Heimlich maneuver on a dog, hold him with his back against your chest and your arms around his waist. With your hands at the dog's upper midabdomen (just behind the last rib), make a fist with one hand and grasp it with the other hand. Quickly thrust up and in with the fist four or five times. This forces a burst of air through the larynx, which should dislodge the object.

Chapter Seven: Vet Care for Your Vizsla Dog

Deep Cuts or Lacerations

Stop bleeding as described above. When bleeding has stopped, clean the area around the wound with povidone iodine or chlorhexidine to reduce the risk of tetanus or other infection. Be sure not to touch the wound with either product, as they can sting and irritate the skin. Then flush the wound with tap water until it looks clean. Don't rub the wound with anything — not even a gauze pad — or you could start the bleeding again. When the edges of a wound gape open or when cuts or lacerations are more than ½ inch long, the veterinarian should close the wound with stitches.

Electrocution

Chomping into a plugged-in electric cord or coming into contact with downed wires can cause burns or even death from electric shock. If you find your Vizsla unconscious near an electrical outlet, never touch the dog. Shut off the main power and pull the plug. Then administer rescue breathing or CPR as needed. If CPR is effective, take the dog to the veterinarian as soon as possible for further treatment.

Dogs that are shocked but don't lose consciousness may cough, have difficulty breathing, drool, or have a strange odor in the mouth from electrical burns. Take them to the veterinarian. Mouth burns from electrical shock can heal on their own, but some dogs develop an ulcer at the burn site. If the ulcer doesn't heal, it may need to be removed surgically.

Chapter Seven: Vet Care for Your Vizsla Dog

Heatstroke

Too much activity on a hot, humid day can lay your Vizsla low with heatstroke. Supervise your Vizsla's activity level in the dog days of summer, and make sure he always has plenty of fresh water and access to shade if he's outdoors. Never leave your Vizsla shut up in a car or truck on a hot or even a sunny day. Even if the windows are cracked and the car is parked in the shade, temperatures can reach dangerous levels in a matter of minutes.

Signs of heatstroke are heavy panting and difficulty breathing. The tongue and mucous membranes appear bright red. Your Vizsla may drool thick saliva or start vomiting. Body temperature can rise to 104°F or higher. If left untreated, the dog goes into shock, collapses, and dies. Never let the situation become this dire.

At the first signs of heatstroke, move the dog into an air-conditioned area if possible and begin cooling him with cold water. Bathe him with wet towels or use a spray bottle to wet him down. You can also place the wet dog in front of a fan to help lower his temperature. Take the dog's temperature every ten minutes. When the temperature falls below 103°F, you can stop cooling the dog and dry him off.

Take the dog to the veterinarian as soon as possible. Heatstroke is associated with breathing problems, seizures, and other serious conditions, which can develop hours after the dog has seemingly recovered.

Chapter Seven: Vet Care for Your Vizsla Dog

Hypothermia and Frostbite

Just as heatstroke is caused by extreme heat, hypothermia and frostbite result from extreme cold. Hypothermia is excessively low body temperature. Frostbite, which often accompanies hypothermia, occurs when a part of the body — usually an extremity such as a paw or ear — freezes.

The Vizsla's coat helps protect it from hypothermia. Nonetheless, puppies and old dogs, dogs submerged in cold water for long periods, and Vizslas without the correct coat can fall victim to this condition. Signs of hypothermia include shivering, lethargy, and a body temperature below 95°F (remember that a dog's normal temperature range is 100 to 102.5°F). To treat hypothermia, warm the dog by wrapping it in blankets. Dry wet dogs thoroughly. Call the veterinarian if the dog's temperature is below 95°F.

Suspect frostbite if your Vizsla's skin looks pale white or blue. Apply warm compresses to the frostbitten area until the tissue begins to regain color. Take the dog to the veterinarian as soon as possible. You may have heard that it's a good idea to massage frostbitten areas or to rub them with snow or ice, but that's not true and can cause further damage.

Insect Bites and Stings

Bees, wasps, and other insects can inflict stings or bites that cause allergic reactions. These reactions can include hives (raised circular areas on the skin), swelling, rashes, itching, and watery eyes. Minor reactions, such as a rash or itching can be treated with calamine lotion or a paste made of baking soda. Ice packs help reduce pain and swelling.

A bite or sting on the face or neck can cause dangerous swelling that closes off the dog's airway. Anaphylactic shock is a systemwide reaction characterized by agitation, diarrhea, vomiting, difficulty breathing, and collapse. Any time your Vizsla has these signs, take him to the veterinarian immediately.

Poisoning

Vizslas will eat just about anything on the off chance that it might be food, and poisons are no exception. Snail bait, putrefying animals, garbage, drugs, rodent poisons, antifreeze, household medications, plants, and insecticides are all sources that can poison your Vizsla. Here's what to do if your best efforts at Vizsla-proofing your home and yard fail.

If you see your Vizsla eat something that you know or suspect is toxic, the first thing to do is to confirm what its ingredients are. Look on the label or call the National Animal Poison Control Center. Depending on the substance, you may be advised to induce vomiting by giving the dog hydrogen peroxide. The usual dose is one teaspoon for every 10 pounds the dog weighs. Give the appropriate amount every twenty minutes, up to three times, until the dog throws up. After the dog vomits, give a 5-gram tablet of compressed activated charcoal from your first-aid kit. The activated charcoal prevents absorption of any remaining poison in the dog's stomach. Take your dog to the veterinarian for further treatment.

Chapter Seven: Vet Care for Your Vizsla Dog

Antifreeze has a sweet taste, and antifreeze poisoning is common in dogs. Signs of antifreeze poisoning are depression, vomiting, and seizures. The dog may have an uncoordinated walk, as if it's drunk. If you see these signs, take your dog to the vet immediately.

Do not induce vomiting in the following instances:

- When the dog has already thrown up.

- When the dog is unconscious, convulsing, or having problems breathing.

- When the dog has swallowed an acid, alkali, cleaning solution, household chemical, or petroleum product.

- When the dog has swallowed a sharp object.

- When the label on the substance advises against inducing vomiting.

Some poisons are absorbed through the skin. If your Vizsla comes in contact with a toxic substance, flush the area with water for thirty minutes, then bathe the dog in lukewarm water. Be sure to wear plastic or rubber gloves to protect yourself from the poison.

If your Vizsla gets into the garbage or eats a dead animal, he can suffer bacterial poisoning. Suspect garbage poisoning if your Vizsla appears to have a stomach ache, has bad breath, vomits, and has diarrhea. Garbage poisoning can

Chapter Seven: Vet Care for Your Vizsla Dog

be fatal, so don't hesitate to take your Vizsla to the vet if he shows these signs.

Signs of poisoning may not become apparent for several days. Suspect poisoning if your Vizsla is weak or shows signs of internal bleeding, such as nosebleeds, or bleeding from the mouth or rectum. Take him to the veterinarian immediately. If possible, bring the packaging of the suspected poison with you.

Puncture Wounds and Animal Bites

Puncture wounds are caused by sharp, pointed objects, such as nails, barbed wire, or jagged pieces of wood. Treat a puncture wound the same way you would a bite wound. As long as you clean the wound promptly, your Vizsla shouldn't need a tetanus shot.

If another animal bites your Vizsla, it's important to clean the wound as soon as possible. Bite wounds are chock full of bacteria from the other animal's mouth. If you know your dog has been bitten, stop any bleeding and then clean the wound with povidone iodine or an 0.05 percent solution of chlorhexidine, a disinfectant that's effective against bacteria, viruses, fungus, and yeast. If you suspect the animal that bit your dog was rabid, notify your veterinarian immediately. If the bite is severe, your Vizsla may need stitches. A course of antibiotics can help ward off any infections.

Don't attempt to treat a snakebite by sucking out the venom, making cuts over the wound, applying ice, or washing the wound. All of these actions are either dangerous to you or can make the situation worse.

Vizslas that spend a lot of time in the field are at risk of snakebite, as are dogs that live in areas where snakes are common. Teeth marks in the shape of a horseshoe usually indicate a bite from a nonpoisonous snake. An exception is a bite from the venomous coral snake, which also leaves a horseshoe-shaped mark. The bite of a poisonous snake leaves fang marks (one or two bleeding puncture wounds in the skin) and usually causes pain and swelling. Signs of poisoning from a snake bite include restlessness, panting, drooling, vomiting, diarrhea, an uncoordinated gait, shallow breathing, and shock. Left untreated, a bite from a poisonous snake can kill a dog.

If your Vizsla is bitten by a poisonous snake, keep him still to prevent the venom from spreading too rapidly. Carry the dog if you can, and get him to the veterinarian as quickly as possible for antivenin, supportive treatment, and antihistamines.

Chapter Eight: Showing Your Vizsla Dog

Showing your Vizsla is a great way to build your relationship with your dog and it can be an enjoyable challenge. In order for your Vizsla to do well in conformation he must meet certain breed standard requirements set forth by the AKC, the UK Kennel Club, or whatever breed governing body that is sponsoring the show. In this chapter you will learn about Vizsla breed standards and tips for showing your dog.

Chapter Eight: Showing Your Vizsla Dog

Vizsla Breed Standards

The breed standard is simply a list of characteristics, the ideal specimen of a particular breed should embody. Breed standards are published by breed governing bodies like the American Kennel Club and the UK Kennel Club. Breed clubs like the Vizsla Club of America may also have their own version of a breed standard. If you plan to show your Vizsla you will need to become very familiar with the breed standard because it is the list of characteristics against which he will be judged. You will find a summary of the AKC Vizsla breed standard below:

General Appearance

The general appearance for the Vizsla is that of a medium-sized, short-coated breed with a distinguished hunting dog appearance and bearing. The dog is robust but lightly built; agile and energetic; with a brawny or sinewy muscular condition.

Temperament

The Vizsla is a natural hunter with a good nose and above-average trainability. The dog is lively but well-mannered and demonstrably affectionate. Shyness and timidity should be penalized.

Head and Skull

The head is lean and muscular, the skull moderately wide between the ears with a median line down the forehead. The ears are thin and silky, the muzzle square and deep.

Chapter Eight: Showing Your Vizsla Dog

Legs and Body

The body is strong and well-proportioned with high withers. Proportions should be balanced with a moderately broad/deep chest and well-sprung ribs.

Tail and Coat

The coat is short, smooth, dense and close-lying – no woolly undercoat. The tail is set just below the level of the croup and docked one-third off.

Color

The coat color should be golden rust in varying shades; saddle markings are common. Pale yellow or solid dark mahogany colorations are faulty.

Size

The ideal male is 22 to 24 inches high and the ideal female is 21 to 23 inches high. Disqualifications for males over 25 ½ or under 20 ½ and females over 24 ½ or under 19 ½ inches.

Faults

Disqualifications include: partially or completely black nose; solid white extending above the toes or anywhere except the fore-chest; distinctly long coat

Chapter Eight: Showing Your Vizsla Dog

What to Know Before You Show

If you plan to show your Vizsla dog, there are a few things you need to know before you register. The exact rules and requirements will vary from one show to another, so pay attention to specific requirements.

Before you attempt to show your Vizsla, make sure your dog meets the following general requirements:

- Your dog needs to be fully house-trained, and able to hold his bladder for several hours.
- Your Vizsla needs to be properly socialized, and able to get along well with both humans and other dogs.
- Your dog should have basic obedience training, and he should respond consistently to your commands and look to you for leadership.
- Your Vizsla should be even-tempered, not aggressive or hyperactive in public settings.
- Your dog needs to meet the specific eligibility requirements of whatever show you are participating in. There may be certain requirements for age, for example.
- Your Vizsla needs to be completely up to date on his vaccinations so there is no risk of him contracting or spreading disease among other dogs at the show.

In addition to considering these requirements, you also need to make sure that you yourself are prepared for the show.

Chapter Eight: Showing Your Vizsla Dog

The list below will help you to know what to bring with you on the day of the show:

- Your dog's registration information
- A dog crate and exercise pen
- Food and water bowls for your dog
- Your dog's food and treats
- Grooming supplies and grooming table
- Trash bags for cleanup
- Any medications your dog needs
- A change of clothes for yourself
- Food and water for yourself
- Paper towels or rags for cleanup
- Toys to keep your dog occupied

Preparing Your Dog for Show

Your preparations for the dog show will vary according to the type of show in which you have entered. If you enter an obedience show for example, perfecting your dog's appearance may be less important than it would for a conformation show. Before you even enter your dog into a show you should consider attending a few dog shows yourself to get a feel for it. Walk around the tent where the dogs are being prepared for show and pay close attention during the judging to learn what the judges are looking for in any given show. The more you learn before you show your own dog, the better off you will be.

Chapter Eight: Showing Your Vizsla Dog

One of the most important things you need to do in preparation for a conformation show is to have your Vizsla properly groomed so that his coat is in good condition.

Follow the steps below to groom your Vizsla in preparation for show:

1. The night before, give your Vizsla a thorough brushing then trim his nails and clean his ears.
2. Give your dog a bath and dry his coat thoroughly before brushing him again.
3. Once your dog is clean, you need to keep him that way. Have him sleep in a crate that night and keep him on the leash during his morning walk.
4. The day of the show, brush your Vizsla's coat again.
5. When you arrive at the show, keep your dog in his crate or in a fenced exercise pen so he doesn't get dirty.

When it comes time for judging, just remember that the main reason you are doing this is to have fun with your dog. Do not get too upset if your Vizsla does not win. Just take notes of ways you can improve for the next show and enjoy the experience you and your dog had together that day.

Chapter Nine: Breeding Your Vizsla Dog

The Breeding Process

Age

It would be best if you took note of the proper breeding age for your dogs. A male dog should be twenty-four months old, and a female dog should be at least eighteen to twenty-four months old. The female dog should be eight years old or younger. Although the age recommended for retiring a dog is between five and six years old, it depends on the breed and health condition of the female.

Chapter Nine: Breeding Your Vizsla Dog

Suitable time for mating

Female dogs, days eleven to fourteen of oestrus, increase the breeding rate. Time them when they are already on heat.

Consider their environment

The environment when mating should be quiet, clean, and familiar to male dogs for them to have a compelling performance. Avoid crowded spaces.

The male should not be too obese and should not be too different from the size of the female dog.

Before selecting a breeding partner, it is best to understand its health status. It is not recommended to mate dogs with infectious diseases, genetic history, or close relatives, especially dogs with contagious diseases. They will cause infertility and even cause death. Also, it is best to target an experienced dog to make the mating behavior more smooth.

Different breeding methods can be selected according to the breeding conditions, level, and breeding purpose. For example, free mating consists of putting the selected male dogs into a certain number of female dogs. This enables to raise them in groups and allows them to mate, improving the success/pregnancy rate. Assisted mating (adapted to first mating male/female), Artificial insemination are the most known methods.

Chapter Nine: Breeding Your Vizsla Dog

Introduce the dogs to each other and let them get used to each other. Although the mating process can be speedy, you should not rush it. It may take several hours or days for dogs to adapt to each other. How much time you need to rely on depends on the dog's mating experience, its nature, and the duration of breeding attempts.

Shave the hair under the bitch's tail. This increases the dog's chances of mating, mainly when you breed long-haired dogs.

Check to see if the male dog is sniffing the back of the bitch, and if the tail is pulled in front of the dog. Sniffing shows that males are interested in the females. He can also lick her vulva and try to mount her when she appears kind and ready.

Supervise the dog at any time to ensure its safety. Keep the dog on the leash and the bitch on the muzzle (soft muzzle), especially if she is a virgin.

Talk to the dog in a soft, encouraging voice to make sure they feel confident and relaxed. If you are frustrated or annoyed by a failed attempt, please don't yell at the dogs or lose your cool.

If she is not standing, please grab the bitch. If males are interested in her, she may be too excited or distracted. To keep her still, you can place her head between your legs and grab her with your hands. Then you can move her so that she is in front of the male.

Another person can block the tail.

Chapter Nine: Breeding Your Vizsla Dog

If it is difficult for the male to penetrate, use a lubricant. For example, you can apply petroleum jelly to the vulva of a bitch. Don't try to manipulate male genitals.

Some people try to hold the male and place the penis to achieve maximum penetration and prevent injury, but this can be a little grotesque for new breeders.

Don't worry if the bitch is vocal during pairing. In the first part of the coupling, the female can express her discomfort. In this case, she will need extra comfort. You can talk to her in a soothing voice.

If the dog tries to separate itself during the coupling process before the body is coupled, it could cause severe injuries. Therefore, please hold the female headers during the connection process to ensure that they will not separate.

After the dog ejaculates, the swelling will reduce, and the female dog's vaginal muscles will also relax. Then, the dogs will be able to separate from each other safely.

Sexual Problems In Dogs

Male dog sexual inhibition (inability to erect/asexual impulse)

Insufficient nutrition and exercise, lack of sexual experience, frequent mating in a short period, rough error management, incorrect sperm collection operation, pain, interference, and other reasons can cause sexual inhibition and even impotence.

Lack of sexual experience

Some female dogs struggle to mate due to a lack of sexual experience (especially if they have never been in contact with male dogs). As a result, they might be unwilling to mate even if the oestrus period is reached (heat). At this time, the Breeder's assistance is needed. You could grab the collar with one hand and drag it with the other lowering the abdomen. This helps the male dog enter.

Male dogs, because they have no experience, will crawl without an erection or have no sexual behavior. They might be unsure of the correct position and will have to go through many attempts. Breeders are advised to be patient and gentle to not cause sexual inhibition in male dogs.

Some reasons why the female dog might not get pregnant after mating are brucellosis, infectious diseases, lethargy, swollen lymph nodes, difficulty in walking, vaginal discharge, and testicular swelling. These can cause spontaneous abortion of pregnant female dogs and cause male and female dogs to suffer infertility.

Other infectious diseases may include toxoplasmosis, subclinical uterine infection, systemic virus or protozoan infection, and many others.

Prostate problems (male dogs)

Difficulty in urinating and walking, lethargy, and bleeding from the penis are common symptoms in male dogs for prostate problems. This affects ejaculation volume and sperm motility and is the main cause of infertility.

Hormonal Disorders or Hormonal disturbances in female dogs

Female dogs can suffer from persistent oestrus, schizophrenia, and hypothyroidism, deterring them from producing puppies.

Frequent breeding

When male dogs repeatedly mate in a short period, it results in a decline of sperm quality.

Lack of adequate preparatory stimulation can lead to low ejaculation, poor sperm motility, and inability to get an erection. For example, you can let male and female dogs play together and chase for some time before mating. It improves the quality of sperm and can help release luteinizing hormone and increase testosterone concentration in the blood.

Also, thyroid insufficiency, hypercortisolism, pan-herpes virus, ovarian insufficiency, chromosomal abnormalities may lead to inability to conceive successfully.

Chapter Nine: Breeding Your Vizsla Dog

Few Precautions To Take

Give the female and male dog time to get acquainted with each other and their environment; this helps avoid the female dog being unaccustomed to refusing to mate.

According to the female dog's age and health status, three births in two years or one birth per year are more appropriate. Still, too many births will affect the female dog itself and the health and quality of the puppies. It is recommended to be sterilized during the second oestrus to prevent breast cancer and other diseases and prolong life.

Male dogs are not suitable for frequent mating (for each mating, they can rest for 2-3 days at least), which will affect their health and sperm quality. Therefore, they should not be bred if they are over 12 years old.

Drinking water or strenuous exercise is not recommended immediately after mating.

First oestrus (first heat) female dogs are not suitable for breeding because they become mothers earlier than they should. Most times, they begin to show unpredictable behavior during pregnancy and after giving birth. They act unsure and uncertain of how to behave in their motherhood stage, which is risky because they won't be careful with their puppies, which might endanger them. After the female dog mates in oestrus, there will still be blood flow out until the end of the oestrus.

Chapter Nine: Breeding Your Vizsla Dog

In the case of menopause, older dogs also have the chance of conception, but the conception rate will decrease with age.

During the mating process, attempt to calm the dog's feelings and ensure that the dog is quiet and comfortable. After the mating is successful, do not permit the female dog to urinate within 30 minutes (you can put together a small container to stop her from urinating). Let the sperm continue to be in the female's body for some time, as long as feasible to expand the conception rate.

If you want female dogs to mate with male dogs, try to reduce the reproduction frequency as much as possible. The intermediate breeder level does not mate for at least one season. You should do this to ensure that the bitch can rest and regain her strength. Females who frequently reproduce usually give birth to pups that have a higher mortality rate.

"Stuck" for a long time after the mating

There will be a " stuck " phenomenon when the male dog successfully inserts his penis into the female. The two glands on both sides of the penis will begin to swell in the vulva. The duration is about 10 to 30 minutes or even more sometimes. Wait for the male dog to be calm for some time, then separate naturally. If the dog is in pain, the Breeder can patiently soothe it (touching, talking) to prevent the dog from twisting and struggling due to pain, which will cause the pain to worsen.

Sometimes female dogs can get aggressive during the "stuck" period, trying to twist or run. This will hurt both dogs and result in injuries for life, plus a costly trip to the veterinary. When mating, you have to be present and make sure the female is calmed and not trying anything physically too aggressive. You could hold the female and try talking in a soothing way until they separate themselves.

Do not try to interfere. It will cause infertility or even death if interrupted abruptly. Some of the injuries in male dogs are penile injury, penile bone fracture; in female dogs, vaginal smooth muscle strain, vulva injury, uterine suspensory ligament injury, uterine shedding.

Health Factors To Consider Before Mating

Remember that certain health checks, such as hip and elbow dysplasia checks, can only be done before the dog is at least two years old. However, these tests are very important, so they should be performed before breeding your dog.

Look out for possible health dangers for your dogs. Each breed must have unique potential genetic and health risks. For example, some species like the Vizsla can inherit sight infections. A breed like the German Shepherds often mourns from genetic hip dysplasia.

You are also required to examine the pedigree to find out if your dog has other health issues rapidly.

Chapter Nine: Breeding Your Vizsla Dog

Examine your dog's sightings. A veterinary health practitioner has to look into your dog's eyes annually for current retinal atrophy, which can lead to total blindness and retinal dysplasia. Also, check eye anomalies, cataracts, hereditary, and entropy. A dog's eyelids fold inward or outward.

Make sure your dog has the temperament suitable for its breed. Specific behavioral tests have been developed for common breeds, such as the WAC test for Dobermans. However, a variety of behavioral tests are also provided for all dogs. These tests can indicate the dog's temperament and training level.

If your dog has behavior problems perceived as aggressiveness, irritability, or a tendency to bite, please do not breed them. Likewise, if the dog is shy or submissive, it should not be reproduced.

Breed dogs suitable for breeding are happy, confident, obedient, and well-behaved when interacting with other animals.

Keeping and breeding dogs with behavioral problems have led to the deterioration of many dog breeds, such as Doberman Pinschers and Vizsla dogs.

Ensure that both females and males are tested for brucellosis before breeding. Brucellosis will eventually lead to infertility of both sexes. It may cause a litter of pups to abort or die shortly after birth.

Chapter Nine: Breeding Your Vizsla Dog

Confirm that the males and females are healthy before breeding. Females need to be healthy to withstand the stress and hardships of pregnancy. So don't hesitate to ask other dog owners to provide medical information if you are mating one of your dogs with others that are not yours.

The vaccinations for both dogs should be up to date.

Weaning

Weaning is a crucial segment of puppy upbringing. Whether the puppies are cared for by their mothers or raised as orphans, the method and timing of weaning have lifelong consequences in the Puppy. In addition, mastering to wean can aid a puppy to develop emotionally and socially.

Time is a crucial part of weaning. Three weeks after they are born, adult dogs usually start avoiding puppies and stop breastfeeding. At this moment, the puppies naturally show a reduction in breastfeeding time. Instead, they put in more time studying their new world. This is the time to offer food to them. Even if the puppies are trained as orphans, they should start feeding "solids" at three weeks old. At this stage, gentle treatment of the individual can help develop them physically and socially and make them more presentable and acceptable to human beings.

Chapter Nine: Breeding Your Vizsla Dog

Food

Start feeding the puppies from 3 weeks old, as I have said before. Put a small amount of soft food in a shallow bowl for the puppies. So far, the baby dogs drink to get food, and now they need to learn to open their mouths and bite things before swallowing food. Learning to do this results in a little sloppy consumption time. Puppies usually run and fall on the food tray, putting their paws inside bowls and making a complete mess. In the end, they will learn regular eating habits.

Feed several times a day, about 30 minutes each time. When the little guys are no longer interested in food, clean them up and give them back to the mother. During this time, the mother moves away from the baby. Some mothers and some babies may not wean properly. Mothers who have not yet started weaning their puppies by four weeks of age need help. The weaning process is supposed to be slow to reduce stress and inflammation index on the mother's breast.

Remove the baby several times a day for 1 to 2 hours each time. Food can only be provided for a short time and not left there for later. Still, the separation of the baby from the mother can encourage natural weaning. As the pups get older, more time should be taken away from their mothers until the puppies live alone and are entirely independent of their mom.

By the time puppies are around eight weeks old, they should be eating solid foods.

Conclusion

A Vizsla dog is a truly delightful breed of dog. Aside from being classically beautiful dogs, they are highly intelligent, versatile, easily trained, loving, loyal, curious, playful and they make wonderful companions.

Many Vizsla dog owners are familiar with the quizzical sideways-head turn and the look of sheer intelligence in their eyes as they try hard to grasp what you're saying to them. Their quirky, inquisitive nature means they can be a lot of fun when they play or when they just want to be a little goofy with you.

It's unfortunate that some people seem afraid of these gentle giants. Negative impressions are formed through fear, usually after meeting a badly-trained or completely untrained dog with no control. A poorly trained Vizsla dog may become confused and a little difficult to handle, but with the right attention and discipline it can become a great family pet.

Always take time out of your busy day to spend some quality time together with your dog, either playing or just being goofy. Daily walks are essential with this breed of dog, for both mental and physical stimulation. Grooming should also form an important part of his care and can help to strengthen the bond with you if you treat his grooming sessions as a big affection-giving session.

No matter how busy you are or what excuse you think of not to give your dog the things he needs, remember this:

Conclusion

You have the TV, your computer, your work, your friends, the phone and a myriad of other things to keep you stimulated.

Your dog has only you.

Be all you can be for him. Spend time forging a bond with your Vizsla dog that consists of love, trust and understanding and you'll have a best friend for life.

Glossary of Terms

Adoption – A process in which a rescued pet is placed into a permanent home.

Acute Disease – refers to a disease or illness that manifests quickly

Agility – This is a sport in which the dog handler guides and instructs the dog through a course of obstacles while being timed. Accuracy through this obstacle course is paramount. The dogs must complete the obstacle course without a leash or toys (or food) as incentives. The handler can only use voice, movement and various body signals in order to direct the dog.

AKC – American Kennel Club, the largest purebred dog registry in the United States

Almond Eye – Referring to an elongated eye shape rather than a rounded shape

Apple Head – A round-shaped skull

Balance – A show term referring to all of the parts of the dog, both moving and standing, which produce a harmonious image

Beard – Long, thick hair on the dog's underjaw

Glossary of Terms

Best in Show – An award given to the only undefeated dog left standing at the end of judging

Bitch – A female dog

Bite – The position of the upper and lower teeth when the dog's jaws are closed; positions include level, undershot, scissors, or overshot

Blaze – A white stripe running down the center of the face between the eyes

Board – To house, feed, and care for a dog for a fee

Breed – A domestic race of dogs having a common gene pool and characterized appearance/function

Breed Standard – A published document describing the look, movement, and behavior of the perfect specimen of a particular breed

Buff – An off-white to gold coloring

Canine- a term for dog.

Canine Teeth- also known as eye teeth, the largest teeth found in the dog's mouth. They are long, curved teeth on either side of the mouth, top and bottom.

Chronic Disease – refers to a disease that will last indefinitely.

Clip – A method of trimming the coat in some breeds

Glossary of Terms

Coat – The hair covering of a dog; some breeds have two coats, and outer coat and undercoat; also known as a double coat. Examples of breeds with double coats include Shiba Inu, German Shepherd, Siberian Husky, Akita, etc.

Condition – The health of the dog as shown by its skin, coat, behavior, and general appearance

Crate – A container used to house and transport dogs; also called a cage or kennel

Crossbreed (Hybrid) – A dog having a sire and dam of two different breeds; cannot be registered with the AKC

Dam (bitch) – The female parent of a dog;

Dock – To shorten the tail of a dog by surgically removing the end part of the tail.

Double Coat – Having an outer weather-resistant coat and a soft, waterproof coat for warmth; see above.

Drop Ear – An ear in which the tip of the ear folds over and hangs down; not prick or erect

Entropion – A genetic disorder resulting in the upper or lower eyelid turning in

Fancier – A person who is especially interested in a particular breed or dog sport

Fawn – A red-yellow hue of brown

Glossary of Terms

Feathering – A long fringe of hair on the ears, tail, legs, or body of a dog

Groom – To brush, trim, comb or otherwise make a dog's coat neat in appearance

Heel – To command a dog to stay close by its owner's side

Hip Dysplasia – A condition characterized by the abnormal formation of the hip joint

Inbreeding – The breeding of two closely related dogs of one breed

Kennel – A building or enclosure where dogs are kept

Litter – A group of puppies born at one time

Markings – A contrasting color or pattern on a dog's coat

Mask – Dark shading on the dog's foreface

Mate – To breed a dog and a bitch

Neuter – To castrate a male dog or spay a female dog

Pads – The tough, shock-absorbent skin on the bottom of a dog's foot

Parti-Color – A coloration of a dog's coat consisting of two or more definite, well-broken colors; one of the colors must be white

Glossary of Terms

Pedigree – The written record of a dog's genealogy going back three generations or more

Pied – A coloration on a dog consisting of patches of white and another color

Prick Ear – Ear that is carried erect, usually pointed at the tip of the ear

Puppy – A dog under 12 months of age

Purebred – A dog whose sire and dam belong to the same breed and who are of unmixed descent

Saddle – Colored markings in the shape of a saddle over the back; colors may vary

Shedding – The natural process whereby old hair falls off the dog's body as it is replaced by new hair growth.

Sire – The male parent of a dog

Smooth Coat – Short hair that is close-lying

Spay – The surgery to remove a female dog's ovaries, rendering her incapable of breeding

Trim – To groom a dog's coat by plucking or clipping

Undercoat – The soft, short coat typically concealed by a longer outer coat

Vaccine – a shot that is given to a dog to help produce immunity to a specific disease.

Glossary of Terms

Wean – The process through which puppies transition from subsisting on their mother's milk to eating solid food

Whelping – The act of birthing a litter of puppies

Index

A

aggression 100
allergies 34, 113
anal sacs 63
appearance 150, 172
award 171

B

bark 90
bathing 54
behavior 5
behaviors 79
bitch 173
biting 87
bleeding 138
body 174
bones 125
breed standard 150
breeder 10, 18
breeding 155
brush 55

C

cage 172
canine 115
canned 36
castrate 173

Index

certificate 17
chewing 92
children 5, 14, 25
choke 141
clipping 60
coat 4, 52, 151, 173
collar 22
color 4, 151
coloration 173, 174
colors 174
comb 173
come 68
command 173
companion 8
condition 173
contract 11
crate 77

D

dam 172, 174
dangers 24
dental 60
diet 32
diseases 109
disorder 172
double coat 172
dry food 37

E

ears 57
eating 175
emergency 131
epilepsy 130

Index

exam	114
exercise	5, 50, 158
eye	7

F

face	171
fat	29
feed	46
feet	59
female	4, 156, 171, 174
first-aid	131
food	27
foot	173
foxtails	119

G

gene	171
genealogy	174
genetic	172
groomer	52
grooming	4, 51
growth	174

H

hair	174
harness	22, 95
health	6, 107
healthy	11, 110
hip	173
hip dysplasia	126
homemade	42

Index

hot spot 119
house 171, 172
houseplants 26
howl 90
hunting 4
hygiene 62

I

illnesses 107
injury 114

J

jumping 94

K

kennels 19
kibble 31

L

label 39
leash 22, 94
lie-down 69
lifespan 6
litter 175
lumps 112

M

male 4, 156

Index

markings	174
mating	156
menopause	162
milk	175
mineral	32
mouth	61
mouthing	87
muzzle	133

N

nail	7, 59
neutering	108
nose	7
nutrients	27

O

obedience	66
obesity	50
oestrus	161
outer coat	174
owning	16

P

parent	172
performance	44
personality	108
poisons	145
potty	74
preparations	153
prostate	160
protein	28

Index

puppies 175
puppy 11

R

record 174
requirements 152
rescue 12
reward 87

S

safe 24
showing 149
sire 172, 174
sit 67
size 3, 15
skin 28, 173
skunk 63
socialization 17, 98
spay 173
spaying 108
stay 73
supplements 46
surgery 174

T

tail 172
teeth 23, 60, 112, 171
temperament 3
toenails 58
tools 53
toys 23

Index

training 66
treats 47, 78
trimming 171
trust 89

U

undercoat 172

V

vaccinations 110
veterinarian 111
vitamin 32
vomiting 121

W

water 31
weaning 165
weight 4, 50
whine 90
wounds 147

Index

Photo Credits

Page 3, csabap via Canva.com (Canva Pro License)

https://www.canva.com/photos/MAC8t2ANnoU-vizsla-puppy/

Page 10, Bang via Canva.com (Canva Pro License)

https://www.canva.com/photos/MADT4L8OQUE-vizsla-puppy-playtime/

Page 21, Akivegzo Images via Canva.com (Canva Pro License)

https://www.canva.com/photos/MAEB4ubqQ18-hungarian-vizsla-puppies/

Page 27, Akivegzo Images via Canva.com (Canva Pro License)

https://www.canva.com/photos/MAEB4rxRbUE-hungarian-vizsla-puppies/

Photo Credits

Page 51, Akivegzo Images via Canva.com (Canva Pro License)

https://www.canva.com/photos/MAEB4g3SEjE-hungarian-vizsla-puppies/

Page 66, Hobli via Canva.com (Canva Pro License)

https://www.canva.com/photos/MAC6cTjiKfc-vizsla/

Page 107, RRUEL via Canva.com (Canva Pro License)

https://www.canva.com/photos/MADpBbMMAoc-vizsla/

Page 149, PharmShot via Canva.com (Canva Pro License)

https://www.canva.com/photos/MADNnxrK4Ok-vizsla/

Page 155, anikalauerphotos via Canva.com (Canva Pro License)

https://www.canva.com/photos/MADWCmzfI7A-vizsla-puppies-sleeping/

References

American Kennel Club n.d, AKC, accessed 5 December 2021, https://www.akc.org/dog-breeds/vizsla/

Animals Network Team n.d, accessed 8 December 2021, https://animals.net/vizsla/

AZ Animals 2021, accessed 5 December 2021, https://a-z-animals.com/animals/vizsla/

Canna-pet n.d, accessed 26 December 2021, https://canna-pet.com/breed/vizsla/

Dogbreedslist.info n.d, accessed 10 December 2021, https://www.dogbreedslist.info/all-dog-breeds/vizsla.html

Dogtime.com n.d, accessed 8 December 2021, https://dogtime.com/dog-breeds/vizsla#/slide/1

Dr Gemma Gaitskell n.d, Dogzone, accessed 22 December 2021, https://www.dogzone.com/breeds/vizsla/

Embrace Pet Insurance n.d, accessed 10 December 2021, https://www.embracepetinsurance.com/dog-breeds/vizsla

Espree n.d, accessed 22 December 2021, https://www.espree.com/BreedProfiler/vizsla-grooming-bathing-and-care

References

Gemma Johnstone 2019, TheSpucePets, accessed 5 December 2021, https://www.thesprucepets.com/vizsla-dog-breed-profile-4775723

Hill's Pet Nutrition Inc n.d, accessed 7 December 2021, https://www.hillspet.com/dog-care/dog-breeds/vizsla

Katie Mills Giorgio 2021, Daily Paws, accessed 5 December 2021, https://www.dailypaws.com/dogs-puppies/dog-breeds/vizsla

Kidadl Team 2021, accessed 15 December 2021, https://kidadl.com/animal-facts/vizsla-facts

Kiki Kane n.d, Rover.com, accessed 27 December 2021, https://www.rover.com/blog/12-things-might-not-know-vizslas/

Lifetime Pet Cover n.d, accessed 22 December 2021, https://www.lifetimepetcover.co.uk/pet-advice/dog-breeds/hungarian-vizsla/

Michele Welton 2021, Yourpurebredpuppy.com, accessed 11 December 2021, https://www.yourpurebredpuppy.com/reviews/vizslas.html

Nicole Cosgrove 2021, Hepper, accessed 16 December 2021, https://www.hepper.com/vizsla/

Orvis n.d, accessed 10 December 2021, https://www.orvis.com/vizsla.html

References

PDSA n.d, accessed 8 December 2021, https://www.pdsa.org.uk/pet-help-and-advice/looking-after-your-pet/puppies-dogs/large-dogs/hungarian-vizsla

Petcloud 2020, accessed 18 December 2021, https://www.petcloud.com.au/d/blog/hungarian-vizsla-dog-breed/

Petfinder n.d, accessed 15 December 2021, https://www.petfinder.com/dog-breeds/vizsla/

Petinsurance n.d, accessed 22 December 2021, https://www.petinsurance.com/healthzone/pet-breeds/dog-breeds/vizsla-dog/

Purina n.d, accessed 18 December 2021, https://www.purina.co.uk/find-a-pet/dog-breeds/hungarian-vizsla

Vetstreet n.d, accessed 22 December 2021, http://www.vetstreet.com/dogs/vizsla

The Kennel Club n.d, accessed 5 December 2021, https://www.thekennelclub.org.uk/search/breeds-a-to-z/breeds/gundog/hungarian-vizsla/

Thomas 2020, Medpaws, accessed 18 December 2021, https://www.madpaws.com.au/blog/vizsla/

References

www.ingramcontent.com/pod-product-compliance
Lightning Source LLC
LaVergne TN
LVHW051831080426
835512LV00018B/2813